Revelation in the Wilderness

Revelation in the Wilderness

By Kenneth Del Vecchio

ISBN: 1-58820-066-3

To my wife, Francine. The person who completes me.

PREFACE

The wild winds blow and the canyon echoes howl with a spray of acidic dust and ancient artifacts. Green is black. And black and white are gone. Alone, he stands as man's first and man's last, looking out at the desolate ruin of populace, idly monitoring the ash of concrete jungle, human indiscretion and innocent wildlife species. It is apocalypse now.

For years, he had traveled. Sometimes alone, but more often in groups. He had tasted the flavors of life, embracing its duality of hollow body and body of soul. He had intertwined intimacy in both positive with negative and positive with positive. He had shared in laughter and in love and struck out in sorrow and in anger. His passions for the tastes of wine and the miracles of water had fruited for him a cascade of knowledge and scholarly successes. He never knew what it was all about, though. His journeys. His experiences. His learnings. Nothing had showed him. His tenure in the militia, however, ultimately brought about his realization. For it was there, where he learned of killing.

He knew that wars were fought on beaches, upon hills and mountains, and on and under oceans. He had heard of battles in open fields, in dug-out trenches and throughout the open skies. But this combat was carried out in the wilderness. Fighting was on this physical ground, the war though, battled in the beast of the mind.

The Medicine Man, as he was known to the other troops, was able to leap several prongs of the military ranks because of his schooling as a physician. He was an officer, a designated leader by right of formalized hierarchy. This was something his travels had taught him made no sense, but nonetheless was a truism in the mechanics of a wartime fighting regime. Another truism, was that leadership was also a growth from skill and courage--inherent traits almost immediately attributed to the Medicine Man by the others. They all looked up to him, heard him, listened to him. But the listening, he saw, really mattered none.

Out in the wilderness terrain, it was a frost bitten drudgery of solitude and massacre. The sole matter was death. There weren't any other problems. In this field of nightmares, there really weren't any but that singular one. There were no niggers or kikes or wops or spics. No right wings or leftists. Or pimps or whores. There were no homos or hippies. Not a Roe, nor a Wade. Right to life wasn't even heard of. Right and wrong, neither.

In the wilderness, he had bucked high with the bulls and pawed down with the bears. He had carried men from and into eternity. He watched as the cream of insanity dribbled from one man's lips, across his cheek and down his chin. And then met with his limb, engaging to his utmost extremity, where by his own hand, he took his own life. There, in the beast of the wilderness, there weren't any rules or guides to go by. But the Medicine Man spoke words of service anyhow.

To subordinates and superiors alike, he was a prophetic statute of language of morals and strength. He only hesitated to speak, because he, same as the others, was a conscious actor in the commission of the seven deadlies...but he spoke to them. "We must all be wary of our pending destruction. Today, here, cover yourself with arms. Tomorrow, in the hereafter, let your arms cover others with love."

They heard, listened and they killed. They killed, because they had to. They were ordered to. They had been ordered to for thousands of years. For excavated ruin after ruin proved it. History explained it. Present preserved it. Future will perpetuate it. So the orders will keep coming. There, in the wilderness, he knew this to be true. And he, himself, carried on with it.

Forty Battle Days Later

"Sir...Sir?" A youthful fair skinned, fair haired company man whispered at his externally opposite doctor-mentor. The Medicine Man did not respond to him. He was in a slumber of sorts, uncomfortably resting his eyes and psychosis, much the same as nearly all the others in the unit. The boy wanted to talk. He wanted to sleep too. But he couldn't. Not that it was his watch. But it was always *his* watch. It didn't seem right to him to sleep. For himself, for everyone else he now lived with, he didn't feel right sleeping. The Medicine Man wouldn't respond, though. So the boy closed his eyes...

In the distance, he heard the pitter-patter of his baby brother's rattle. Pit pat. Pit pat. Pit pat. Pit pat. And then, closer, he heard the loud booming of his stereo system, which he thought he had shut off because it was night time. He never left it on during the night. And his mother never raised a hand to him before. So it was strange. And it awoke him when her fist cracked him across the skull...

The doctor dove atop the boy when the flashes of the night showed him the teenager's face explode to allow an enemy bullet inside it. He ripped open the child's shirt and stripped down a piece of the uniform to temporarily tie his head back together. The screams all around him ensured that many others had been wounded as well. The clarity of those screams also ensured him that this young man was now dead. Nothing, no sound, no breath rose from this individual's mortal being any longer. The boy soldier's watch was over.

The Medicine Man scurried to his field supplies. Tourniquets. Stitching. Metal tools. Drugs. Into the dark, he carried his trade, intending to follow the screams of the night. But instead, the naked kernels of human ecstasy curdled in his blood, and he out lashed with a vengeance at the mocking foes on the other side of the line. He raced in terror at the adversaries, piercing human cavities with knives and pellets. Dismembering and beheading the tormentors of his kind. His kind. His kind?

And now, he is not there in the wilderness. He is here. In the barren wasteland. The desolate, lifeless world he chose to create. Adam cried out, alone as he was. "It couldn't work! It can't work! From day one to day last, I couldn't work it out. Nor could she. Nor could they. None of us can ever be what we are suppose to be. Never."

So by his choice, by his singular determination, they all died. The evil. The good. The weak and the strong. The men, the women and the children. All of them. In one blast of immortal order and seizure, the entire lot of human invention was annihilated.

Today, in the wasteland, it is over. For the third and final time, he leaves for home. He leaves as man. And returns home as man's maker.

CHAPTER 1

(One Year Earlier)

What do you say about someone who tormented you in love? Who tortured you with obsession? A man who brought you to an end, yet gave it all up for you. Do you begin with the end? Or do you begin with the beginning?....I'm not sure. I think you just begin.

The day Adam Burr proposed to me was normal, uncelebrated in every way. The sky was clear, yet cloudy in plotted areas. The temperature was midway, somewhere between warm and cool. I had begun work at nine and ended at five. Adam hadn't arranged for a quick getaway vacation to Florida or one of the islands. There weren't even plans to meet at an expensive restaurant. He was just having dinner with me at his parents' home in suburban North Jersey, a region of the Northeast United States which is separated by crossing paths of distinct highways and similarly converging cultural communities.

I remember the dining room table--an antique oak woodwork passed down from Adam's great-grandmother to his grandmother to his mother. A 14 foot piece, it centered the room, erected quietly in the charming, dimly lit eatery. This was the benchmark of the maiden side of Adam's family--wealth and class, touched with modesty.

I sat at that table idly...waiting. Just waiting. I didn't know for what. But I just knew there was something that night. I remember feeling Adam hovering over me. I felt his broad shoulders and his powerful chest. I couldn't help feeling uneasy. But somehow, I felt incredibly safe. He spoke to me quietly so his parents couldn't hear. "Are you satisfied with me? With our relationship?"

"After three straight years of monogamy, I better be...Of course I am."

"Then perhaps it's time," he said.

"Time?" I guess I was confused. I often was with Adam. I could never figure out exactly who he was or what he was going to do.

"Please accept this ring as my request for your hand in marriage." Adam was so calm, yet so sexy.

The proposal was an enigma. An aberration on all counts. Adam had never talked about, even intimated, the idea of marriage. And if I had ever expected the proposal, I would've never expected it to be so formal....You see, Adam Burr was an outrageous personality. He was a "one-and-only". He was wild, a bar room fighter. But intellectual, both in writing and oration. Adam could beat you physically and mentally. Through strategy, manipulation, force. Sometimes, even through humor. He could laugh you into a loss. A stoic request for life-long unity was the last thing I expected--I accepted on the spot.

Afterwards I thought about how I felt when we first started dating.

In the garden where fair children play, words become messages and messages become law. The law of the loved is to provide love, and love will abound and circle to the hearts of the many who call to its kindness.

Today, I can't say that I'm in love. I can't say that I'm even close. I don't know enough yet. But there's something about the words he uses when he speaks. The choices he makes. The charm and the grace in the manner he says the words he says. The way his lips move and how his eyes brighten. The words themselves actually mean something to me. Not usual, I admit. But it's the unusual that attracts me.

Some time ago, not long ago, I met him. Not by coincidence. It was arranged. He sat by me, close to me, and spoke to me. But not really to me. Nor did I really speak to him. We kind of, truly I guess, carried on a conversation. And for some time, I would say. Yes, we spoke a lot, but learned nothing of each other. But still, his words meant a lot to me. True, in this case, in this first meeting, his words meant a lot for reasons of my own ego, which I don't feel compelled to explain. But in short time, his words meant a lot for other, more sound reasons.

Following the promises of the charitable domain and promising the same as it is warranted and expected, the exact light of the rainbow and the true shadows of Mars, Jupiter and Venus can be seen through a kaleidoscope of terms and messages. They can be seen in another person's words. His words in conversation of mores and politics, entertainment and fun and just simple talk about nothing much, somehow, in their totality, makes me feel like it is right. But you can't ever know until you know. So I don't know. And I've told myself that. But his words keep coming. And his smile, there's fate in his smile.

This is a rare man. Believe me, once, just once before, I had a rare man. And in the most serious way. And I can tell you, a rare man is most distinguishable. It's not by a mark or a look or a shape or a kind. It's by that unique design of unapproachable qualities of intellect and wit, ambition and strength, and charisma and beauty.

I'll admit, and quite pridefully, that I've held in my arms many a strikingly gorgeous man. Perhaps because of a unique design of my own, perhaps just by pot luck. In any case, it has happened. But in every case, but one, it's been meaningless. And I pray for meaning, so I pray for a second coming. An even better coming, I hope. And is it here? His words are letting me know.

In the garden where fair children play, the top will spin and the wheel will turn, and destiny will determine where it stops. A force of equity will bind together all those who are fair and just, those who receive and give love. The true loves will learn from the words in the garden and will gain from the words of the mate. So spin the top and turn the wheel, but don't make it stop. Let it stop. When love from the words really lets you know.

His words really had let me know. They had showed me his

3

intellect, his emotion, his kindness. They had showed me his intense love for me. And in turn, the intense love I had for him. I was proud to spend the rest of my life with this man. And eager to unravel all the mysteries that surrounded him.

CHAPTER 2

Charles Sutton was a long way off from law school. He was even years away from his infamous criminal defense practice. He was happy, though, that he could still work for his clients. The work was just different. A lot different.

The exiled attorney removed a lengthy screwdriver from his waist. It was the same screwdriver he had used the night before for the Princeton University lab break-in. A straight edge with a shiny yellow handle. At the lab, he needed much more than this primitive tool, however. A computer decoding device to disarm the alarm system and automatic door locks. Two .44 caliber bullets to kill the lone security guard. And vast medical knowledge to isolate and remove the necessary goods.

The pay for the night before was good. Twenty-five thousand cash. The pay for this day was equally as good. As it would be for several upcoming visits. Sutton's disbarment was what caused the need for nonlegal fees. But his disbarment wasn't what caused his desire to carry out these new duties. It was simply hate, anger and insanity. His clients, now his bosses, coveted these ill feelings. And they coveted the insanity. The insane mind of a genius, as Sutton was, could yield incredible results. That made the twenty-five thousand per incident well spent. Especially in this project.

No one saw the tears in Adam's eyes. We all could see his emotion and intensity, however. Even though he hadn't spoke one word of his summation yet. A once promising young physician known for his wartime quick suture heroics, Adam was now known for his powerful and passionate lawyering. For his seemingly flawless legal arguments. Today, he knew he had to meet this reputation and more.

Although I prosecuted for the office that Adam was defending against, I rooted for his victory. I watched his late thirties toned, athletic body rise from counsel table. His long strides allowed him to reach the jury box in only a few steps. Each jury member, he made eye contact with. This was not a jury of his client's peers.

Eight men. Not one of them a homosexual, he was certain. Adam had wanted more women because they would be more sympathetic to his client, Frank Yome. But the jury pool was overloaded with men and Adam's peremptory challenges ran out. This left him with what he knew was probably an intolerable group. Intolerable to Frank Yome, a gay man.

Yome's homosexuality could not be brought out in trial. It was not relevant to the case. But his homosexuality was evident. No one could miss it. The way he moved. The way he spoke. The way he looked. This was definitely a gay man. And gay people were not accepted by most of Bergen County, the county where this jury came from.

The case had received a lot of press. Not because the charges were incredibly serious, but because of Yome's presence in the wealthy, basically crime free community he resided in. Frank Yome was not your normal homosexual man. He cross-dressed, was especially out-spoken and was the son of a very powerful individual. A very powerful man whom Adam had previously successfully defended against racketeering, extorsion and gambling charges. Bergen County residents didn't like Frank Yome, Sr. And they didn't like Frank Yome, Jr either.

Although Adam knew the jury was not suppose to know of Frank Jr's homosexuality or his family's criminal indiscretions, he knew they did. Junior's charges of cocaine distribution were all over the news. Adam liked the publicity, though. He liked the adversity. He actually even personally liked both Frank Yome, Senior and Junior. And he genuinely thought Junior was innocent, unlike Senior. This belief exhilarated Adam and I knew it was what caused the tears to fill his eyes.

Charles Sutton's screwdriver was used to pry open a screen. That's all. Once the screen was off, Sutton lumbered his overweight two-hundred and twenty pound body through the open window. He went straight to the room's bed which held his victim. A young, beautiful woman, laying without covers in her night clothes, taking a mid-day nap. Her large breasts were barely held in her scant Victoria's Secret negligee. Her thick, long light blond hair lay to each side of her pillow. Sutton peered for a moment at the girl's sultry, sexy body. His excitement was evident in his almost black eyes. The young woman saw it when she awoke. Her momentary scream was blocked out by a quick jerk of Sutton's left hand, forcing a moist rag into her nostrils and mouth. Sutton died out any struggle she could have put up. He spoke one word as she was passing out. *Slut.*

Adam's tears dissipated as he moved an easel in front of the jury box. On the same, he affixed a large piece of construction paper where he wrote REASONABLE DOUBT in black marker atop it. He had told me earlier that he felt the State had numerous weaknesses in its case where it was impossible for the Prosecutor to meet his burden of proof--to prove Frank Yome is guilty beyond a reasonable doubt. But mere factual dissertation of doubt would not be enough for an acquittal here. Adam had to embrace the jury with fury and make them feel the injustice that could be done to Yome, and thus to anyone, if the constitutional mandates of reasonable doubt were not adhered to. His oration would be crafty, but loaded with common sense. Adam blinked an eye at Frank, Sr who was sitting in the front row of the court room. His emotional voice began as he pointed at the assistant prosecutor from his position beside the easel.

"Per se reasonable doubt. You know what that is? It's one person's word versus another's. And that's all we have here. Nothing else. No testimony from anyone but the arresting police officer. No fingerprints. No video tapes. No tape recordings. No motive. There's nothing to show that my client dealt cocaine except one police officer's word. A word which is backed by nothing. And on top of it all, my client has an alibi...Is this a case where the prosecutor has proved guilt beyond a reasonable doubt?" Adam, who had been resting his hands on the oak frame of the jury box, suddenly turned away and went over to the prosecution's counsel table. He peered at the state's representative. "Is that what you're going to tell them when you speak? That you've proved guilt beyond a reasonable doubt?"

Adam shook his head with a mock nod and moved back to the twelve men and women he had been speaking to. "Over here, to my right, is a chart. In a moment, I'm going to go over twenty facts, undisputed facts, listed on this chart. All which have been brought out in this trial and all which prove my client's innocence and show more than reasonable doubt. But before I do this, I ask you, I beg you, to hold one cannon in your mind. One passage of justice..."

That was the beginning of Adam Burr's twentieth consecutive successful closing argument, which only hours later resulted in a Not Guilty verdict for Frank Yome, Jr.

Not many hours after that, Charles Sutton was guilty of a very serious crime. And he was long gone from Princeton. But his legacy hadn't left the posh New Jersey town. A prominent university laboratory had been burglarized. What, if anything, was stolen, no one could ascertain. A former police officer, working his years of retirement in the serenity of an easy security job, was dead. And a pretty college student had been sexually assaulted.

Jessica Jamison, an ambitious Florida import, ending her first Ivy League semester, wasn't the woman she was the day before. Late in the night, she found herself strewn out across the floor. Completely naked. And violated. Bruises were all about and inside her. On her chest. Arms. Back. Head. Legs. And vagina. Her buttocks were not bruised. But they were not left alone. A single word was hand painted upon her cheeks. *AIDS*. And by her side, was a short typed note which read:

...With my other eye, I looked into the heavens, spotting the angels and the other characters floating effortlessly in the

8

winds. But my eyes weren't enough. They never were. So I sought the aid of the canals in my head that allowed me to hear the whispers down below. Through them, I derived peace and comfort and was provided with directives.

CHAPTER 3

From the Bible:

Then I saw in the right hand of him who sat on the throne a scroll with writing on both sides and sealed with seven seals. And I saw a mighty angel proclaiming in a loud voice, "Who is worthy to break the seals and open the scroll?" But no one in heaven or on earth or under the earth could open the scroll or even look inside it. I wept and wept because no one was found who was worthy to open the scroll or look inside. Then one of the elders said to me, "Do not weep! See the lion of the tribe of Judah, the root of David, has triumphed. He is able to open the scroll and its seven seals."

Adam appeared to not be listening, probably because he already had knowledge of the story. Instead, he ran his hand gently upon the side of my leg, then pinched my thigh.

"Ouch," I whispered and laughed, "Are you crazy, we're in church."

The old lady who always wore a scarf and carried two bags glared at me. She sat next to Frank Yome, Sr, who was oblivious in his make believe world of morality. "I'm sorry," I mouthed to her, then turned back to Adam who was still playing with my leg. "We're in church."

"Do you think God really cares if I fondle you a little bit? He purposely gave us all a sex drive. And more important, he gave you and I a sex drive toward each other. Why? Because he wants us to procreate. He wants the human race to continue and thrive. And exist in his image. And his image obviously has a sex drive. So, he wants us to play a little. Even in his house. You see, we'd be slapping Our Father in the face if we didn't fool around a bit in here." Adam managed to say all this in the same whisper voice I embraced. The old woman now had a permanent glare in her eyes, beaming in our direction.

"God, it's not like I'm cursing His name. I love Him." Adam

shrugged his shoulders at the old lady.

I grabbed his hand. "Listen to the Bishop," I told him.

"I always listen to the Bishop." Adam sat back in the pew.

The tall, slim man at the podium wore a meter, a large triangular shaped hat. Underneath it, and barely visible, was a zucchetto. This bini type head piece attached to his scalp and was the same light color as the larger hat. A black cassock fell over his entire body. Its scarlet buttons and piping highlighted the otherwise plain robe. A scarlet belly band finished off the fabric part of the high priest's outfit. The man, though, was otherwise distinguishable as a Bishop via his pectoral cross, which signified the office. Of course, you couldn't miss the gold ring shining God on his right hand.

Bishop John McFarlane was the head of St. Anthony's, his church. And he was the head of the Burr family. He had been a second father to Adam, there in his life right from birth. He was the brother of Adam's mother and he was Adam's personal confidant--the only person to whom the entire ordeal of the war had been revealed.

Adam referred to him just as Bishop, at least for the last seven years he had. Before that, it was Monsignor. And before that, Father. The earlier years, he was Crazy John. It was a strange nickname for a man who held one of the Catholic Church's highest offices, but you never know what people were like in their younger days. I knew what the Bishop was like now, though. He was a sensational speaker, a man who could tell a story. No matter how boring the story would've been with someone else telling it, it was exciting hearing it from him. Scripture was fascinating. Homily was captivating. Even saying the Hail Mary with him was somehow better.

Yes, the man had an effect on people. Adam, most of all. He always wanted to please the Bishop. But he wouldn't always do what the older man wanted. He wouldn't attend church every week. He wouldn't abstain from pre-marital sex. God knows, Adam wouldn't do that. And he wouldn't run for the open

United States Congressional seat that Bishop wanted him to. But he did listen to him. And now, he was doing just that. Together, we heard and thought about the words.

Freedom to choose one's will is the ground beneath the feet of each American man. No, it's the ground beneath each man. The will to choose is grounded within all, beginning in the Hall of Souls, from the Old Soul to the New Soul to the New Born Man. But choice may be available more or less from country to country. And likewise from man to man. And from man to man is the will to be free...and hopefully the will to free all from the Hall of Souls to become New Born Men.

Mass ended with the Body and Blood of Christ and final words to go in peace. We had shook hands with our neighbors, Frank Yome, Sr and his wife and the old lady with the two bags. And we had pledged, in our thoughts, the happiness to all we loved and maybe to those whom we did not love as well. After everyone else had departed the Catholic chapel, we met with the Bishop in a room adjoining the rectory.

Inside, we sat cattecorner to each other at a wide marble top table. Laid out across the same were assorted pastries and juices, flanked by unlit odorless candles and various plastic flower arrangements. The windows were open, though, permitting the fluttering sounds and airs of nature to reach our senses.

The Bishop picked out a raspberry tart and began to question Adam. "Back in the arena, huh?" He meant church.

"It was her idea," Adam smugly responded, pointing at me.

"No it wasn't," I started, but quickly realized how that might sound. "I mean, you know I always come, but Adam wanted to be here. His heart is telling him to come back." Adam glared at me like the old woman had during mass. He couldn't look long, however, because the Bishop was already on to another subject.

"So what's your plans with the election?" he asked.

"I'm going to support--"

The Bishop cut Adam off. "Why support? You've been

nominated to run...again."

"Haven't we had this discussion? I think at least twenty times."

"Twenty's a bit of an exaggeration, wouldn't you say? But that doesn't matter. What matters is that you need to be motivated. You're a leader. You've always led. Everybody wants you to lead."

"But I don't want to run again now. It's not that I don't want to hold office, Bishop. I just don't feel it's time now. I need to build my resume more."

I laughed at that. Apparently the Bishop found it funny as well.

"Are you a joker? You're a graduate of medical school. Of law school too. You held a state assembly seat at twenty-five. And you're a war hero. Everyone wants to see you in Congress. That's why your party nominated you."

"Well that's another thing."

"What?" The Bishop was becoming impatient. His bouncing fingers on the table were a tell-tale sign.

"I'm not sure this is *my* party. I mean, what's the difference between parties anyway? I'm so tired of this partisan crap. If you name me any politician, just pick a name, and I'll tell you exactly how he'll vote on any issue. You know how I can do that? Because of partisan politics. None of these people think on their own. They just vote with the party, every single time on every single bill. There's no individuality. There's no real voice for their constituents."

The Bishop's fingers were still bouncing. "Are you finished?"

"Not yet?"

"What else, Adam?"

"I already gave my word that I would support Susan Sezman."

The Bishop's fingers weren't bouncing any longer. They were now balled up in a fist. "Are you insane?" He slammed his closed hand into the table, cracking his ring upon the stone face and causing me to jump back. "That woman...that woman...is pro-choice. She's an Anti-Christ."

"But she's an individual." Adam held a slight smile. He stood up from his seat and came behind me, resting his hands on my shoulders. I shivered a little at this moment, fearing that Adam was going to use me as an example. My pro-choice stance was not a secret to the world, nonetheless I didn't want to share this view with the Bishop. My apprehension was relieved quickly however, as Adam spoke in an effort to remedy his mentor's angry reticence.

"An act of abortion is an atrocity. Without fail, in each and every case it's a sin against God. It's the willful prevention of a human life by other human beings. It's a choice no person should make."

"So you listened to my homily," the Bishop stated, referencing his earlier church talk.

"Of course I listened." Adam was now massaging my shoulders, I don't know why, and blowing down the nape of my neck.

"And we've talked about this before." The Bishop was observing Adam's antics. "What in God's name are you doing?"

"Acting in God's name is exactly what I'm doing." Adam had departed from the massaging and instead was caressing the back of my head.

"Do you want me to leave the two of you alone?" I interjected, desiring to avoid this growing ordeal.

"No," both men simultaneously answered. Accordingly, I determined to stay put, but rather than involve myself in the actual argument, I drifted into my own related thoughts.

A caricature of the Bishop, bent and standing on one leg, presented itself in my subconscious conscious. His triangular hat had become a circle, never ending and always the same. His cross was doubled, two-sided. And his ring was broken in pieces, laid out neatly on the table. Still, I heard his words, even through this jumbled mess. They made sense and seemed right, although I disagreed with the outcome.

Isn't the choice of what to do with one's own body a fundamental right? Hasn't our society, our own Constitution, in fact determined that choice is law? And what about a woman who is raped? Or what if the birth of a child that no one ever knew meant the death of a woman dearly loved? Should men be able to make this decision for women?

The Bishop's caricature hopped from one end of the table to the other. His circle spun around his head, not totally unlike a halo. He chomped at a few sentences in Latin and picked out the Bible for a passage. He cited the birth of Christ and the Holy Mother's tremendous burden of raising such an important and controversial boy. Could anything have been more difficult, he asked. If the Virgin Mary had tainted her never touched womb and acted on her environmentally, human-given *rights*, and killed the Son of God, before he had a chance to be born and suffer for the sins of all mankind, would Susan Sezman even be here to assert her United States constitutional laws? How about the laws of God? Don't they count?

I counted from one to a hundred. And then counted the same numbers backward. I said the alphabet twice, then picked out all the vowels and lined them up from *a* to *u*. And then recited the fifty states and all their capitals, only forgetting that Cheyenne was the state seat of Wyoming.

The Bishop puckered his lips and blew a streamline of chilled breath at his broken ring, causing it to tumble and turn and piece itself back together. It rested motionless for a beat, shimmering and shining, then sailed through the chill to the hollowed hands of its owner.

Through the mist of my mind, I watched Adam's mouth move. For once, I couldn't hear his voice, but I knew what he was saying. He was justifying his anti-abortion views in face of the fact that he defended men who committed murders. And in face of the fact that he himself had killed during the war.

Man killing man is only permissible in God's eyes when man is defending the life of fellow man. Man defending man who kills another man is a necessary evil in the world that man lives, a world which God chose to create. Sometimes, though, an accused man is not a man guilty of murder at all. And saving that one man from death by the hands of another man, which is the capital punishment of an innocent man, makes the defending of all accused men the Word of God.

Watching Adam's mouth move in synch with God's word, I again became desirous to hear his actual speech. I channeled my full energies back into the conversation to decipher its final results. Adam was finishing a monologue about considering the totality of a person. The good versus the evil. And how it's all a weighing process. The Bishop was biting his tongue, reluctantly accepting the outcome of their discourse. He knew he had won the war--Adam was opposed to abortion--but he had lost the battle. Adam still was not running for Congress this year and he definitely was going to support Susan Sezman.

I noticed during our ride away from St. Anthony's that Adam was silent. I know, what's to notice when someone is silent? And it's not that Adam is never silent. At times, he is quite quiet. But why be silent now? He was just in a great mood, touching and playing with me. And he had just stood fast against the Bishop's dictates and demands. He held his own against the most persuasive, the only persuasive, man in his life. So, why then the damn silence?

Adam flipped the radio volume from mute to a loud volume. Moments later, it was returned to mute. Something was coming, I knew it. So I initiated whatever it was before he could. "What's your problem?" I asked.

"My problem is that after all this talk about improper behavior by women, I started to think." Adam accelerated, moving into the fast lane.

"Does that mean you have to speed and drive carelessly?" I pointed at the automobiles we were inappropriately passing on the highway.

"No, you're right, Laura. It doesn't." Adam slowed a bit, but continued with his problem. "Forget the abortion issue, I've had enough with that," he paused, "But I just can't stand the fact of what you would've been willing to do as an actress."

This was something Adam Burr was infamous for. Bringing up some irrelevant fact or even nonfact, from the past. The same topics, over and over again. How he loved to beat them to death and me right along with them. But there was no point to it all, because he never changed his position and I never changed mine. I viewed the arguments as a stressful waste of time. I think he kidded himself that we were honing our advocacy skills. So the debates, as he called them, would endure. And we would waste time.

This particular issue arose from our first meeting, almost four years earlier. We had met in law school, but not pursuant to our legal studies. I thought I was there to just pass the time while I was waiting to become a successful actress and screenwriter. Adam was there to relieve his mind of the terrors of war and to find a new profession which didn't involve the horrors of human blood and desecrated flesh.

I had drafted what I thought was terrific script, with me playing the lead role of course. To gain momentum and hopefully interest wealthy law professors and alumni to invest, I convened a reading of my work at the law school. I needed actors to bring the screenplay alive, so I sought out friends in the field and eager film wannabees from my classes. But I couldn't find the right man to play opposite of me. I didn't have that handsome, charismatic leading male. Then Adam appeared. He had learned of the reading through another student and he respectfully inquired if I would cast him for the event. Would I? Of course I would.

So there we were. In front of an entire lecture hall of people, reading my words together. Playing off each other, smiling and laughing. Acting out fright and other similar emotions. And romanticizing and fantasizing the love scenes. That was it, that was the problem--the love scenes. Or as Adam put it, the sex and nude scenes.

Adam sped up the car again to get my attention. "Can we talk about this?"

"I thought this was resolved, hmm, maybe three and a half years ago." I was clearly being sarcastic.

"But you still have dreams of being an actress, Laura." He said the word *actress* with patent disdain, like it was a bad word. It disgusted me.

"Do you have a point?"

"Yeah, that means the problem is still alive."

"No, Adam. There is no problem. You just won't accept me as an actress."

Adam took his cue to rip into me. "I accept you as an actress, Laura. But I don't accept that you're willing to flash your chest to a million people...and, God help me here...make out with other guys. That's insane. Are you telling me that those were or are your plans?"

"I never said I would do that as long as I was with you, Adam. In fact, I've always said the contrary." According to me, that should've obviously ended the discussion. But not according to Adam. There was always much more he wanted to add. So I continued just to spite him. "It's not real, Adam. There's no emotion behind film love making. Actresses would never kiss actors if it weren't for the roles in the films. And vice-versa. Kissing someone in a movie is only acting."

"Acting? Are you kidding me?" Adam suddenly departed from the left lane, directly moving to the right lane and then to shoulder where he came to a complete stop. He jerked the emergency brake, ensuring no forward motion. Then he reached over to the passenger side of his vehicle and began passionately kissing me. The special flavors of his kiss caused me to momentarily forget the tensions of our argument. But my forgetfulness was only as long as the moist caress we shared. Adam discontinued the romantic flash with the release of the emergency brake and the tread back into thoroughfare traffic.

"Was that acting?" He was excited now and answered his

own question. "No. That was my tongue actually in your mouth. That's not acting, Laura. And it never is. When two people are tongue kissing, they're tongue kissing. That's reality."

"I don't think you understand reality," I lied to him. No one understood reality like Adam did.

"Sure you don't. And here's some more reality for you. Kissing someone in a movie, getting fondled and felt up--that's prostitution."

"You are totally nuts." I had never heard this argument from him.

"Am I? What's the definition of prostitution? Performing a sexual act that you wouldn't perform unless you were paid for it. Well, as you said, actresses aren't doing it for love...they would never do it, but for the role in the film. They're getting paid for the sexual act--the kissing, the showing of the breasts. They're not getting paid by the Johns--they're getting paid, instead, by the producers. Are you trying to tell me, that in some twisted way, that legitimizes it?"

"I don't have to legitimize anything, because I'm not doing anything." I turned the radio on to listen to some other voices.

Adam ignored the radio and kept on. "But you've contemplated these actions. You, at one time, intended to perform these sex scenes...and intentions are what's important. It's just as bad if you shoot at someone and miss, as if you shoot at someone and kill them. The intent to kill was there both times."

He was comparing me to a murderer; I couldn't entertain this colloquy any longer. I leaned back in my seat and turned my head toward the window. I closed my eyes, striking away light for darkness. I wasn't with the dark side, though. Calm black was just the back drop for my revisiting of childhood songs. *Happy Birthday* met with *Old McDonald* and then with *Ring Around the Roses*. And then *Happy Birthday* again. And again. *Happy birthday to me. Happy birthday to me. Happy birthday to me.*

"What are you doing?" Adam interrupted my black. I

assume he didn't like my silence.

"What are *you* doing?" I returned with the real question.

"What do you mean?"

"You analogize me to a killer? Are you kidding me?" I think my eyes started to tear. For the first time, out of hurt, since I met Adam. "What is it that has stripped you apart? That's made such a good man, such an angry, confused man at times?"

"I'm not angry, Laura. I'm rarely angry."

I turned my head to the window again and saw that we had finally reached our block. It was a perfect block. In dimension. In quality. The houses were clean, well kept and complimentary to each other. They were different sizes, contrasting colors, but still somehow equal to each other. I liked my block. It was right.

Adam down shifted and eased the car into our driveway, parking it. He ran his hand across and around the leather-cased steering wheel and fumbled with the keys dangling from the ignition.

"Adam?"

"Laura?" His voice was gentle as it commonly was.

"I thought I was asking the questions now?" I sort of smiled. I could tell he was going to talk to me.

"When I was fighting, out in the wilderness, there was this kid in our unit. I knew he really looked up to me...Killing and death was the only thing that surrounded us. You didn't care about race or ethnicity or some right to choose. There wasn't any choice out there..."

"Keep talking to me, Adam." His face was drawn. I saw age in him, something I had never seen before. But I wanted him to keep talking, because I thought, in the end, it would make him stronger.

"I do these things, cause these arguments with you...to get away from these other problems. Maybe the war itself. Maybe just fears, I don't know exactly what. It's like there's layers in my mind. One needs to be peeled away from the other. The top layers, I think, are the problems I faxcimilate. They're there to protect me from my unconscious."

I thought about my unconscious and I shivered. I tried to tell him what I knew, though . "It's your unconscious that you need to get to. To learn what you're really feeling. To really learn about you."

"I don't know if I really want to know about me. I don't know if anyone should really know about me. But I think the layers are beginning to peel away anyway, right to the bottom."

The screams of hell rang out. Across our path, a patch of demons danced a web of exhilarated deceit. Red and yellow and fire blew into our bellies and canaled a path to our chests. The Styx of Satan plunged with the fire to break bread into our hearts. But ney, the bells of Heaven sounded with the trumpets of Peter and Paul and John most of all, and ripped away at the tyrannical beast that so dearly wanted to make brethren with our souls. The kingdom, so clearly was theirs.

And to me, that day, Adam imparted the story of the Boy Soldier's watch.

CHAPTER 4

At the crossroads and the corner of the tempest and the ocean, we partners embrace a paradigm of naked success. Encouraged by the whims of the forefathers and the Father, and the instinct to be maternal, we cajole and cover each other with each other with the determination to prosper in ecstasy. We make love divine and therefore divine love.

Adam cuddled up upon me. We had reached pleasure simultaneously and now held the pleasures of each other in our arms. Every time it was special, this time no exception. I whispered to him, "I want to have your child. I want to be the mother of your sons and daughters. And the grandmother of your grandchildren."

"You have my permission," Adam laughed. "And I'll enjoy every moment in getting there." Then he looked me up and down. He turned me over and ran his hand across my back and further on. And then he pressed up against me to peer into my eyes. "You know, you've got the hottest body...and a gorgeous face to go right along with it. Thank you."

"Thank you?" I questioned, blushing.

"Thank you for allowing me to make love to you."

Adam's last words were probably the nicest ever said to me by a man. They were careful, yet spontaneous, and I knew true. I thought about them from the early morning to the evening hours. And I carried them with me to our scheduled engagement with Susan Sezman. I even smiled when I shook her hand, the phony she was. Her pro-abortion stance wasn't enough for me to truly want to support her. Still though, she probably was the lesser of two evils in the primary battle that ensued due to Adam's nomination rejection. Her opponent, Mac Blaine, was a right wing conservative. Lower property taxes was his thing while with the state senate. Okay. But he was an NRA poster boy, a lobbyist's dream on that front. He fought health care reform with a passion. And he did everything he could to foster racial separatism short of calling for crackers to battle coons at public hearings.

Susan Sezman perhaps was an individual. But to me that's what she was trying to be. Her firm handshake only confirmed my conclusion. "So you're the next Mrs. Adam Burr?"

"The next?" I tried to smile right with her, but I fear I frowned instead. Adam came by my side quickly.

"The only one that will ever be." He kissed me on the cheek.

"Well she's a lucky woman. And I'm sure you're a lucky man in the same respect, Adam. I know I'm lucky, very lucky, to have both your support." I know Susan was really directing that statement just to Adam. But why shouldn't she? She was only a viable candidate because Adam declined. And what he brought to the table for her was enormous. Money and votes. There was nothing more a person seeking elected office wanted. Or needed.

Adam excused himself to attend the bar and Susan meandered away to stroke other potential fundraisers and campaigners. She chatted and frolicked with men in suits and women in evening gowns. She talked and talked. To everyone she could who had monetary resources and social power. I noticed, though, how she attempted to avoid Frank Yome, certainly a lucrative financial asset--but more likely a political albatross. It was a wise move on her part; a paparazzi snap shot of the two of them sharing physical graces would mean more than a thousand words to Blaine. But Yome caught up to her despite her maneuvering. I surveyed Susan's response from a distance. She acted cleverly and swiftly, grabbing another male bystander, positioning him between herself and Yome. With manners, she conversed with Yome and the man at the same time, nodding probably at nothing but saying something of political substance nonetheless, I'm sure. Whatever she said, Yome stepped away apparently pleased. He smiled and strolled over to another well dressed middle-aged male. Charles Sutton.

As Yome whispered to Sutton, I caroused my surroundings, wandering from place to place. The rooms were a decorative mesh of ivy and pale stone. And wood and stainless steel fixtures. The floors were waxed and polished and bright with sparkled footsteps of inherited wealth. Large cathedral ceilings with brazen chandeliers hanging from golden rods kept out the rains and thunderous nights. Heavy cast iron doors and laser technology kept out the creatures of those same frightening evenings. This was Susan Sezman's family fortress. The perfect choice of venue to seduce the upper class faction of New Jersey politics.

Adam approached with two drinks in hand, both his as they were vodka mixes. "Where's mine?" I was a bit annoyed. Adam didn't answer. His attention had been diverted in the direction of Sutton and Yome. But not at either of them.

"Is that Mark Weinstein talking to Yome and Charles Sutton?" Adam squinted. His vision wasn't twenty-twenty.

"Yes it is." I only knew who Mark Weinstein was because he formerly was the head of homicide at the prosecutor's office where I worked. He left during my first year of employment because of the state policy forbidding prosecutors from engaging in political activity.

"He's got some balls showing up here." Adam was more than a bit annoyed. "This is invitation only. This is Susan's private residence." Adam walked over to Weinstein, still holding both his drinks, sipping from one of them.

Susan came up to me as Adam walked away. She handed me a glass of wine. "Adam told me you liked Pinot Grigio."

"Thank you." This time my smile was genuine.

"I'm sorry about the *next* Mrs. Burr comment. My timeless struggles with the great, crazy John McFarlane sometimes interfere with the ultimate respect that I have for Adam and all the rest of his family."

"The Bishop's always been a political foe, huh?" I finished my wine with that question. How wild this was. Here I was, a thirty year old, low level lawyer, drinking cocktails with the state's top political operatives and having conversation about a religious icon whom I was closely allied with.

"We have more than politics in our past, Laura." Susan finished her wine.

I didn't know how to respond to that statement, so I pointed to Adam and Mark Weinstein. "How'd he get in?"

"He slithered in." Susan rolled her tongue, making the sound of a snake and stared at Weinstein. "I guess he shook someone down for their invitation." She looked to me. "You think he's got a donation for my campaign?"

"Yeah, sure. I saw him carry in a couple bricks of gold." We both chuckled. "Why don't you kick his ass out?"

"No, no. Let him enjoy my food. Let him be. He can't do much damage here. Most of these people are my friends and already committed to me anyway," Susan thought for a second, "Well, maybe not. Let's go see this prick."

I was starting to like this woman. She had a feisty nature about her. Maybe that individualism Adam saw was real and valuable after all. I followed Susan. I think she wanted to move fast, but instead we kind of sauntered over to Adam and Weinstein. It was more lady-like and it failed to disclose our actual eager interest in the men's interlocution. We passed the bar, the socialite suits and gowns, and Yome and Sutton. That put us right in the mix of the argument already raging between Adam and Weinstein.

"I thought I was the one who was supposed to be doing the debating here." Susan tried to interrupt them, but to no avail.

"You mean to tell me that you want to let all those diseases-ridden, ghetto-filling parasites into our streets? Don't you think we have enough problems in the cities? That's where they'll go, you know. Right into the cities, inhibiting what little productivity is left in them." Weinstein didn't mince words. He said what he thought, not caring who was listening or who was writing down his statements. He was a natural spokesman for Mac Blaine, the reason why the candidate chose him as his

26

campaign manager.

"Are all immigrants really disease ridden?" Adam was mocking and not at all addressing Weinstein's point.

"Come on, Mr. Liberal--"

"Mr. Liberal?" Adam never liked to be classified one way or another. He stepped a notch closer to Weinstein.

"Yeah, Mr. Liberal." Weinstein didn't flinch. "You call for an open door policy of immigration? We don't have enough money, resources or space to let every alien in who wants to strike it rich in America."

Adam had his response ready. "First, I've never advocated an open door policy as you're obviously defining it. You're trying to twist my position for any listeners who may have just joined the conversation and missed my earlier recitation on the topic. To reiterate, I think the government must closely monitor who comes in and when, and the reasons for their entry. But, I do think we must always have a totally open door for any persons who will be killed if they remain in their homeland or if they are returned to it after attempting to flee. Like Haitians."

"Haitians?!" The former prosecutor had a diabolical look in his face. "Haitians? They're the lowest of the alien trash. They're the devil's spawn. And talk about disease-ridden, they're an AIDS infested society of junkies and perverts. Aren't they just the type of people you killed to keep out of our country?"

Adam was startled at Weinstein's last statement. It wasn't apparent to any of the large group that had now gathered. But I knew it startled him. I saw the disturbance.

Buckshot and knives and other stark weaponry burrowed their way to the surface. Swarming bees and circular saws met with colored winds and gregarious fellows. One such fellow opined to know the answer. Strike with the vengeance and force of the engines of war and sting with the venom of the killer bees. But then, an eagle flew out overhead and directed itself to the majesty. And green leaves and flowers carefully, but powerfully, pedaled their way to the firepower, smothering the same with their ferociously sound beauty. A calm set in and the eagle whistled with the other birds. Was the issue resolved? For the moment.

Adam met Weinstein with reserve. But he again refused to directly respond to his adversary's inquiry. "What do you know of death and killing and the reasons why? Don't answer me, because you can't." He took Weinstein by the shoulders and then gently pushed him away. "Debate with Susan now." Adam picked up his two drinks, sipping from one of them as he departed into the crowd.

Charles Sutton apparently enjoyed the show. He snickered at Weinstein and clapped his hands. And he kept clapping. Susan tried to speak above the clanging, but was unable to retain her train of thought. "Would you stop?" She demanded.

Sutton brushed his palm down his neatly trimmed beard and then clapped once more. "I apologize, my old friend. Continue with divesting your platform to us. Please, continue."

I watched Susan turn from Sutton and begin to speak. And I watched Sutton watch her. I listened to her and Weinstein babble on about other foreign and domestic issues and I observed Sutton's growing fury as each subject changed. His face reddened with malice aforethought and his beard bristled with temptation. Each word brought out a darker shade and a stiffer growth. I watched this all until Sutton suddenly departed and Adam appeared in his absence.

Adam waved to Weinstein, distracting him from his current lecture about taxes. "Yes, Mr. Burr? You're back?"

"Mr. Weinstein, I am. And I thought, perhaps we could share a private drink. Let Ms. Sezman carry on in her engagement. You and I, and my lovely fiancee, can adjourn to a private room and maybe we'll orchestrate a public debate between the candidates. We'll talk shop."

"Sure. Fine. Why not." Weinstein looked around for a moment and then stepped down from his fictitious podium. He proceeded with us to the Sezman library.

Inside, Adam sat beside me at large oval table. Weinstein situated himself directly across from us. His balding head acted as mirror to the skylight above, reflecting the moonlight and a few of the galaxy's stars. Adam poured three sifters of aged scotch as he looked at God's night.

"So, what do we discuss?" Weinstein chimed into nothing.

"So what do we discuss?" Instead of resting his hands on my shoulders, Adam placed them on Weinstein's.

"I don't know. What?" Weinstein was uncomfortable. He sort of moved in his chair.

"What about," Adam shifted and wrapped his arms around Weinstein's chest, clasping his hands together, "What about, what you know about death and killing and the reasons why." Adam's voice was moderate but his demeanor clearly was not. Weinstein wiggled, trying to be released from Adam's grasp, but to no avail. "Do you want to get up? Get away?" Adam yelled.

"Let me go, you bastard!"

"Bastard? Now, that's not a nice thing to call me. That's personal." Adam squeezed tighter on Weinstein's chest, hugging him like a bear. "Now tell me, what do *you* know about death and killing and the reasons why? It's not a rhetorical question any longer."

"I know I was too old to fight, to be drafted." Weinstein whimpered.

"No, I don't think so. You're just about the same age as me. Well under thirty-five when things went down." Adam just looked a lot younger than Weinstein.

"Let me go! You're going to finish yourself, Adam. I'm telling you, let me go. Let me go!" At this point, Weinstein was yelling about as loud as he could. And his face was starting to turn from blood red to a pale shade of blue. None of his anguish was discernable to the outside world, though. That good fortune was due to the stone walls and heavy doors. Nothing was leaving this room. But I could see it all.

Here, for the moment, Adam had his folly. And to be honest,

I didn't care what he did. Of course, only anything short of killing, which I did know was not an option.

"Adam?" I did know killing was not an option.

"Yes, Laura?" He was now rubbing his chin into the back of Weinstein's neck.

"Adam?" I did know.

"I'm just trying to show Mark what books can't." Adam uplifted Weinstein from his seat, and then cradled him gently upon the table. Weinstein's head was pinned against his knees, his body contorted between Adam's locked arms. His tie was choked around his neck and his white cotton shirt ripped from his pants. He squirmed and shook, but he couldn't release himself. And he continued to yell to be let go.

"Now you know something of pain and suffering, my tough, tough friend," Adam palmed Weinstein's head, "But you still know nothing of death and killing. And you will never know the reasons why." At that Adam pushed Weinstein away, his body sprawling out on the library table. Adam dropped back a bit and lifted his sifter. He sipped his scotch as Weinstein rolled from the table and ran from the learned room.

A room with a view. Ahh, nothing better than a room with a view. Charles Sutton loved a room with a view just like everyone else.

Paradise. A soft wind and sunshine. A sandy beach, laying naked against a crystal ocean body. Paradise. No! Paradise for Sutton was the body of the naked victim lying in front of him. The forty-seven year old woman's blond hair was the only thing covering herself. It fell nicely upon the left side of her face, leaving the remainder of herself open.

Sutton dropped his screwdriver in his childish knapsack and removed a rag which was only recently submerged in chemicals. He suffocated the unknowing woman and then forced himself, with his pants down, on top of her. No one heard. No one knew. The writing left behind, though, only confirmed the violent and insane nature of this man:

...I shriveled in fear for a moment, watching Igor's brow crinkle and his hand raise. The blow to my head was powerful, but disarming. The fact that he had failed to procure a weapon for his unleashing of punishment meant that my error of judgment was not grave in his calculation. Accordingly, he handled me with judicious discretion, only physically pummeling me to the dirt and fornicating in a manner about me, which to all who did not understand, was atrocious. But I understood, and I accepted the assault with brave obedience.

CHAPTER 5

From the Bible:

Then I heard a loud voice from the temple saying to the seven angels, "Go, pour out the seven bowls of God's wrath on the earth..."

The third angel poured out his bowl on the rivers and springs of water and they became blood...

Then the angel said to me, "The waters you saw, where the prostitute sits, are peoples, multitudes, nations and languages. The beast and the ten horns you saw will hate the prostitute. They will bring her to ruin and leave her naked; they will eat her flesh and burn her with fire."

A serial rapist was on the loose. It was a well known attorney, Charles Sutton, although no one knew it at the time. His method of operation in every case was the same. There was a residential break-in. The victim was chloroformed, disrobed, if not already nude, and beaten. And then sexually assaulted via genital intercourse. *AIDS* was hand printed on her buttocks and a typed passage from a horror story was left by her side.

There were differences, however. Differences in the victims themselves. While each woman was a blond, their ages varied. They were getting older with each attack, in seven year increments. Jessica Jamison was nineteen. The next victim, Marlene Herrera, twenty-six. And then there was Kim Sera, thirty-three, followed by forty year old Cindy Marltana. And finally, just three days earlier, the forty-seven year old, Shirley Windsor, fell prey to an assault.

Every light haired fifty-four year old woman in the state was nervous, strangled in the fear of unknowing. There was no way to know who the rapist would strike out against next. Ethnicity was not a factor. Nor religion or social class. Education had meant nothing, as well as occupation. The rapist's randomness stymied law enforcement's efforts to apprehend the offender.

With no physical evidence or eyewitness accounts, the lack of similar victim background made their investigation increasingly difficult. But there was one connection among the women which law enforcement did not know.

Not far from the railway station located adjacent to my house, is a small park with a pond. In certain months, ducks would swim the pond, paddling with their webbed feet and chattering in obnoxious, squeaking sounds. Their voices could be distinguished from one another though, and if you listened closely you could understand that they were God's creatures. And you could learn from them, if you wanted to, just like you could from all others.

In the water with the ducks were other assorted life, but they were all beneath the surface rather than above where the birds moved about. I couldn't see the various fish and algae and the like, but I knew they were there. And at times, this bothered me. The lack of sight, the lack of real knowledge of their existence was troublesome. But I guess I had to rely on belief. On faith.

I sat on one of the park's benches, pondering the pond and its underwater inhabitants and my faith in them. And I threw bread to the ducks, watching them swat at it with their bills and swallow it into their fluffy bellies. It was early morning this day, maybe seven or eight o'clock, and the weather was brisk. I had wrapped a scarf around my neck and buttoned a sweater over my flannel shirt. My hands were left free and uncovered so I could handle and throw the bread to my seasonal friends.

With one of my hands, I reached into my shirt and pulled at the gold chain I always wore around my neck. I lifted the piece of jewelry from where it rested against my chest and dropped it against my outer clothing. I looked down at it with awkward sight and marveled at its color, and even more so, at the ornament attached to it. I saw an uplifted man with a crown of tears, slightly raised, but pinned against a cross. This ornament was gold like the necklace, but certainly had much more value. I believed in it, although I did not have all the knowledge of its maker. But I did know the exact reason it sat against my heart each and every day.

Adam had purchased the chain for me, as well as its crucifix counterpart. The memory of the day he gave me the gift stood out in my mind with unusual significance. It was the day I graduated from law school, two years from the day Adam had graduated. But it wasn't my graduation or the ceremony or the party afterwards which warranted such significance. It was the way I received the gift.

Adam, his mother and the Bishop sat quietly at a corner table in the restaurant where my graduation party was being held. Their disassociation with the other people was strange, inapposite to their behavior all evening. They had more than interacted with my other guests for the ninety minute cocktail hour which initiated the party. Entertainment, in fact, had been their specialty. The Bishop, in his dark out-of-church suit, played the piano with his sister, while Adam sang lyrics through a microphone. They hit fifties tunes and rock from the seventies. Rhythm and blues melodies and soul classics. Adam's mother even sang a duet with him, a love ballad she had personally written in her early twenties. This was a talented family, and they were a hit with my family and friends. But their social intercourse stopped short when the cocktail hour ended and dinner seating began. From that point on, they sat alone at their table, chatting only amongst themselves.

For the first few moments of their retreat to solitude, I sat with them. There was no more amusement. And no talk of superficial pleasantries. There was only discussion of law and politics. Why the sudden change in demeanor, I didn't know, but the conversation eventually led to Adam's change of career. The reasons why he left being a physician to become an attorney and the role medicine had played in his success in law. He explained that as a doctor, his fundamental task was to treat and better ailing individuals. To actually save them from death in many instances. This was clearly at the core of that profession and, as he later found, at the core of his new profession as well.

Lawyers' responsibility to treat and better the lives of those they counsel is the most basic tenet of their field. And as Adam learned in his particular area of practice, criminal defense, saving clients' lives may be just as routine.

I stayed with them long enough to hear Adam expound on his internal doctor/lawyer relationship because it was new information to me. But when the topic went back to general law, I left them alone to converse. I had other company to attend to and, quite honestly, I was a bit annoyed that they had segregated themselves from my other guests. Everyone else was still standing in groups, not seated at tables, and talking with smiling faces. As I spoke with the others, I glanced over to Adam and his family every so often. And I was finding their behavior increasingly rude. But I ignored my feelings when the Bishop waved me back to the table.

"Laura," he said my name but motioned to Adam, who took out a small box and placed it on the table, "Laura, how old are you?" The Bishop was now looking directly at me.

"Twenty-six."

"Your nationality?"

"Irish and Italian."

"We know your religion." But I knew the Bishop wanted me to say it anyway.

"Catholic." *Is this going anywhere*, I wondered.

"The car you drive?"

"A Toyota Corolla, but I'm getting an Eclipse." *What is this garbage? An interview?*

"And what exactly are your career goals, Laura?"

"I'm starting at the Prosecutor's Office in Bergen County after the bar exam--"

"But what do you want to do there? What are your ambitions? What are you looking to gain from that office?"

I shot up in my chair, straightening out my back. I was much more serious about being an attorney by the time I had finished law school and I knew what I wanted from the Prosecutor's Office. "Well, I want to learn about the criminal justice system, and how to succeed as a litigator...I also..." The Bishop began tapping his ring against the table, interfering with my response. "I also--"

"Yes, Laura? You 'also' what? Spit it out."

He was making me nervous and I couldn't get my thoughts straight. "Well, I also...I have..."

The Bishop began laughing and Adam's mother threw a napkin at him. "He's just playing with you, child." She smiled at me.

I started to laugh a little with them and looked to Adam. "You guys are real jokers, aren't you? I felt like I was being interviewed."

"Who says you weren't." Adam passed the box he had been holding to his mother, who passed it to the Bishop, who made the sign of the cross over it. Then the Bishop passed it back to Adam. Upon placing the box in his pocket, he took me by the hand and led me to the front of the room by the piano and microphone. He lifted the electronic voice enhancer to his mouth and began speaking to my crowd of guests without warning. "Can you guys hear from me again? For a few more moments?"

The voice chatter turned to a low murmur.

"Tonight's a very special night for Laura, and I'm sure for a lot of you as well." Adam moved the microphone to the edge of his hand and began clapping. "Let's all give her a hand. She's going to do some great things as a lawyer."

I turned bright red as all my family and friends started clapping. It seemed as if it were lasting forever, but finally stopped when Adam began speaking again.

"I guess, as most of you know, I've been dating Laura for the past two years. It's been a wonderful time in my life...taking me away from some not so good times." Adam took the microphone away from his mouth, looking out into the groups of people, searching for my parents. When he found them, he continued. "James, Jennifer, you're proud of your daughter, no doubt. And you're lucky to have her in your family. Well today, I want to do something that is going to bring her into my family in a sense...to thank her for all the good she's done for me. For the changes she's made in me."

I thought Adam was going to ask me to marry him, right there in front of everyone. And I drowned in embarrassment and excitement as he dropped the microphone down to reach for the box. But then, instead of a ring, the necklace and cross emerged. Adam held it up to me and spoke without the microphone, but loud enough for all in the room to hear. "This is a gift from me to you. A crucifix touched by my mother and blessed by the Bishop. It signifies the bonding of our relationship," Adam glanced to the Bishop, "I give you God."

I looked to Adam to put the piece of jewelry around my neck, but he placed it in my hand.

"You must accept God yourself, with the placement of his son upon your chest. You must do this by your own choice. By the use of your own hands." Adam blinked at me and then came to my ear where he whispered, "It's a family tradition. A showing of my love...don't mind the religion."

"I like the religion," I whispered back, smiling and with tears in my eyes. And then I clasped the chain around my neck, where it has remained ever since.

The ducks, who had been quiet for the past several minutes began their quacking again as they watched me replace the necklace in my shirt. They yelped and complained, displaying a rather blatant displeasure for the removal of the crucifix from their sight. Their noise reminded me that I had to get home, though. We were having breakfast with the Bishop.

The Bishop cracked open a hard boiled egg. He peeled its outer cover delicately and placed the broken shell in a bowl. Then he tipped the bowl in the trash can which sat beside him and salted the softer portion of the egg. He licked the salt first and then bit into the poultry matter, swallowing it all after only two bites.

I asked him if he was enjoying his breakfast, to which he only replied with a slight smile. I knew he was trying to be pleasant, but something was preventing such true feelings from emerging in the Holy Man.

"Can I ask you a question?" The Bishop began cracking another egg.

"Yes, certainly," Adam answered because the query was directed to him.

"Are you more out of your mind than I ever thought? What are you doing beating up Mac Blaine's campaign manager? A former homicide prosecutor! Are you nuts?!"

Adam stared with no particular look.

"Adam, is this the way a talented, mature man acts? You let out your expression and emotions through outward, open violence that everyone can find out about?"

Adam still didn't answer. The Bishop continued. "If you want to defend Susan Sezman, fine. But do it through words. You have such gifted, powerful words."

"I wasn't defending Susan." Adam, as usual, only offered a limited response.

"Well, what were you doing?" The Bishop dropped his bowl into the garbage can by mistake. Some of the broken shells went with it. Others fell to the floor.

"I don't feel like discussing this. It's not a matter you need involve yourself, Bishop."

"It damn well is, Adam. This guy Weinstein is running around popping off to everyone about this incident. He's talking about filing ethical charges against you."

Adam laughed. "Ethical charges? There's no basis for ethical charges. Maybe he can file a private complaint for simple assault, but there isn't a potential for ethical charges here."

"A criminal complaint of assault is worse--"

"No it's not. It's my word versus his. That's per se reasonable doubt. Who cares, anyway. I couldn't get disbarred for slapping him around a little."

"Disbarred? I don't think you'd get disbarred either. That's not what I'm worried about. I'm worried about the adverse publicity that could come from this. It could affect your campaign."

"What campaign?" Adam was miffed that the Bishop apparently still wasn't accepting that he wasn't running for office.

"I mean future...future campaigns." Egg shells crackled under the Bishop's feet as he pushed back his chair to stand up.

"I've got to meet with your mother." The Bishop leaned into the garbage can and picked out his bowl.

Adam stood up with the Bishop. "I'll come with you." He grabbed the Bishop's arm and ran his hand down his suit jacket sleeve. "Nothing's going to happen because of this idiot Weinstein. He'll be under control about this soon enough. There'll be more important things on his agenda to worry about, I'm sure."

The Bishop shook his head affirmatively, as if he understood. Then the two men turned to me, both attempting to speak at the same time. Their words meshed; the language was sensical, though distorted. I could hear vowels and consonants and rhythms with lyrics. And I could see the joined dialect. It was old, archaic with a fire twist. But then, the fire was put out, splashed not with water, but a lovely bliss. The tempting tones of the new language excited the loins within, beckoning for a decision. Each beckoned all, and eventually all would make that decision. But now was not that time for me. I finished listening, though, clearly recognizing both ends of the spectrum. Then, the language split apart as quickly as it had collided. I kissed both men, one on the lips, the other on the ring. And I advised them that I might meet up with them, one or the other, later.

It was a Monday, so I should have been at work. Instead, I was at home. I rarely took personal days; I didn't like letting my case load build up. But I just needed a day to relax. After the men left, I went into my bedroom and stood at the foot of my bed. I looked up at the ceiling and across its width. Pretty, I thought. I took pleasure in its plainness. Sometimes the plain things made me feel good. There was no danger in them. So after the ceiling, I turned to the walls, but they were only plain in sectioned areas. Spotted about the walls were pictures and ornaments and the like. And they weren't plain. So I just gave up on my dull pleasure and went to the room's largest mirror. I watched myself undress. I removed my sweat pants and shirt, and then bra and panties. I noticed my blond hair. Plain, I thought. But somehow not. Today, it was special—because someone else was looking at it in the mirror as well.

"My hair's blond too," the person said.

I ripped the comforter from my bed and covered myself. I was scared, but not terrified. Uncomfortable, but not embarrassed. The reason for my resulting emotions was because a woman was talking to me. Susan Sezman.

Susan was unusually calm in her manner. But her appearance was disheveled. Her clothes hung loosely, and her blouse was half pulled out of her skirt. Her face was over indulged in make-up and her cheeks appeared swollen. I was confused, so I asked a number of questions at once.

"Susan, what are you doing here? How did you get into my house? What's wrong with you?"

Susan sat herself in a wicker chair which was really in my bedroom for decorative purposes only. She lit a cigarette without asking if it was okay to smoke and then answered me. "I was raped and I'm going to die."

I realized immediately that the law enforcement's investigation into the identity of the serial rapist, was over. Charles Sutton's final victim had been terrorized. This time, he broke his pattern, though. While Susan was a blond and also fifty-four, seven years older than the last victim, she was not at all random. She was Sutton's former law partner and his former lover. Susan had already revealed the entire ordeal to the FBI and they were currently attempting to apprehend her rapist. She wanted to see Adam now.

Susan slumped into the wicker chair and took long drags from her cigarette until she was just inhaling the filter. She had smoked at least half the pack and was dropping the butts on my floor. I didn't attempt to clean them away. I couldn't even speak to her unless she asked me a question. I watched her ignite another cigarette, waiting for the miserable silence to cease. And then it did, when she suddenly emerged from the chair and pulled up her skirt. "You see this," Susan slapped her hand against her buttocks. "This is where he painted that vile word on me. And this," she ran her hand up and down her entire body, "This is where he brutalized me. This is where he infested me with that disease."

Susan reached into her purse and produced a piece of paper. It was an obvious photo copy of a writing; the typed print was slanted and a few black marks stood out at the corners of the page. She read the note aloud to me. "...And I couldn't ignore the whispers. I grabbed Igor by the roof of his mouth and slammed him to the ground. With a heavy wooden mallet, I smashed open his head and crushed his brains with my bare feet. He died easily and that made me feel good..." Susan threw the paper to my floor. "What the hell is this, Laura? What kind of person is this?...I can't believe Charles raped me."

"I'm sorry, Susan. I'm so very sorry." I didn't know what else to say.

"I know you are. I know everyone is. Most people are good people. Most people don't kill other people. Most people don't take others' lives away."

The Bishop's caricature presented itself to me again. I dismissed it quickly though, and brought a pillow over to Susan for her to hold. I swept my palm down her hair and helped her back into the wicker chair. I was amazed she wasn't crying. But maybe she had cried herself out already or maybe the tears were yet to come. In any case, she was a strong woman. She didn't try to hide the attack or her pending demise via the AIDS virus. She didn't try to avoid the upcoming publicity and the disgrace of this rapist being her former lover. No, Susan Sezman wasted no time in letting it all be known. She went straight to the authorities to ensure Sutton's capture and the end to his wretched behavior. She spoke up after settling into the chair.

"Where's Adam? Did you call him?"

"I did. He's on his way." I had momentarily left the bedroom to call Adam during an earlier silent smoke.

"It's his time now. It must be his time. He has to run in my place." Susan hugged the pillow, wedging it between her knees and chest. "He has to run in my place."

In the court yard of a line of Hoboken row houses, three gas and electric workers chatted as they hoisted a rubber coated cable into the basement of one the buildings. Their initial endeavor seemed simple enough and, when completed, they moved around the yard surveying the different homes to determine the best way to accomplish their next task.

They conversed superficially about the City of Hoboken and its distinctions. The birth place of Frank Sinatra. The origin of baseball. Its skyrocketing real estate and yuppie population. They noted its tiny square mile size and the overwhelming number of bars and taverns crammed into it.

As they continued to speak about the bar scene, the oldest of the men gathered up miscellaneous equipment laying about the grounds and his tool chest and headed to the front door of one of the buildings. He buzzed one of the units and waited patiently for its occupant to answer. When no one arrived, he rang up to a second home. This time, he was greeted by an elderly woman in a robe.

"Hi, Mrs...?

"Mrs. Voletinelli."

"Hi, Mrs. Vol-e-tinelli. Did I say that right?"

"Close enough, son. Do I have a problem with my gas heater?"

"No, you don't. It's with one of the other apartments. We really just need access to the basement." The worker pointed to the basement next door. "You see, we've already accessed that basement. Now we need to get into yours."

The old women nodded and held the door open. The other two men, noticing their colleague's entrance, quickly followed.

The three convened in the lobby, waiting for the woman to return to her apartment. Then, they proceeded not to the building's lowest level, but its highest.

The fourth floor of the row house had only three units. The men bypassed the first two, working feverishly as they had been during their ascent to the top floor. Their tool boxes were discarded early on, leaving them with only various pieces of metal. They screwed one into the other, tightening each component with quick jerks of their wrists. And just as they reached the third apartment, their second task was completed. Without a knock, the three men held firmly to their newly assembled ramming device and blasted through the door.

"FBI!" Each man screamed his title and scurried through the apartment. They searched the bedroom, the living room, the bathroom and the kitchen. They looked in the closets, under the bed and even in a small crawl space. But they found no one. Charles Sutton was not home for the law enforcement officers' arrival.

The agents replaced their pistols in their holsters and went through the apartment. It was covered with pornographic pictures and commingled with screened cages of snakes. Other than that though, his home was basically normal. It was clean and neat. And furnished well, with all the average necessities present. The only outstanding item was a note left on the kitchen table. The oldest agent dropped it as quick as he had snatched it up. "Holy shit!" he screamed, looking out to the fire escape from the kitchen window. His two partners ran with him to the outside stairwell, glancing down at the note's message as they passed it by--*I'm right in front of you, you dumb pricks.*

Sutton darted down the fire escape, with the FBI in hot pursuit. Their guns again drawn, they were unable to fire because of children playing stick ball in the back yard. They weren't fearful of striking the children with a direct hit, but rather were worried about the ricochet of bullet fragments. The FBI agents, who were in significantly better cardiovascular shape than Sutton, gained ground on him immediately, however.

But Sutton had his escape route already plotted out. He raced to a rickety wire fence that bordered an old garage and narrowly wedged himself between the two, then pulled a rope which released two garbage cans and other assorted trash from a canopy. His pursuers, forced to momentarily cease in their trail to remove the blockade, lost in the foot race. By the time they were able to pull away the garbage, Sutton was already in an automobile, wildly laughing and making obscene gestures.

The FBI agents/gas men turned to their radio support and notified of Sutton's motor vehicle status. Other FBI were deployed in the fugitive hunt, as well as Hoboken and Jersey City Police.

Sutton calmly traveled down Hoboken's main avenue, Washington Street. He passed the bars and taverns, McDonald's, Dunkin Donuts and Barnes & Noble. The yuppies looked on in interest, though, at the convoy of lit up police cruisers treading on his heels. Sutton ignored the flashing lights and sirens and made a right onto Observer Highway. There, he was met by several more marked and unmarked police vehicles, as he entered Jersey City. These cars, however, came at him almost head on, attempting to thwart his progress.

Sutton changed his method at this time, accelerating to a greater speed. He dodged all the automobiles with uncanny precision, weaving in and out of traffic until he found himself behind a stopped bus. There, he jammed on his breaks, crashing into the back of that vehicle. His head cracked the windshield, but no injuries were suffered. The police in front of him utilized a loud speaker to advice him to exit his car. The police behind him blocked him, not only in the rear, but at both sides as well. Sutton, with no alternative, threw his hands on the steering wheel and waited for the police to arrest him.

After Susan departed, Adam and I drove to his office for an emergent meeting requested by Frank Yome, Sr. I shouldn't have gone; it's not proper for an assistant prosecutor to be privy to a criminal defense attorney-client relationship. Still, I went.

It had been an emotional day and I didn't want to be alone. Apparently, neither did Adam as he asked me to come along.

Yome was already in Adam's office when we arrived. One of the staff had allowed him to bypass the lobby waiting area and ushered him into Adam's private quarters. Yome greeted us with a smile and took our jackets as if he were the host and not Adam.

"I can see that the two of you are upset. Please take comfort in a seat."

"We're going to, Frank. We just walked in." Adam took the coats back from Yome and hung them in his closet.

"How are you, Laura? Adam told me that Susan was just at your house."

"I'm shook up," I told him as I seated myself on Adam's leather couch.

"This is a mess. This whole thing is a terrible mess." Yome pushed back his thick dark hair.

"Are you in trouble, Frank?" Adam wanted to get to the point.

"Me? No, no. I'm not." Yome looked at me as if he were suddenly uncomfortable with my presence.

"She's leaving the Prosecutor's Office in a couple months," Adam lied.

"Okay. Not that I don't trust her, it's just that this is a very sensitive issue."

Adam waited for Yome to continue, still not offering that he would ask me to leave. I was too interested to excuse myself. So we sat for a few seconds until Yome went on. "Susan is a friend of mine. She's a good friend of yours as well, true?"

"I would say so. I intended to give her my full support, and I'm devastated about what happened to her."

"Yes, we all are," Yome agreed.

Adam looked away from Yome and out his window. "It's sick what Sutton did to her. What he did to all those women."

"It's disgusting," I chimed in, "I can't believe he's that demented." I was angry. I knew that Charles Sutton had had problems with the bar and some skirmishes with the law, but I couldn't fathom he would do something so evil.

"These were inhuman acts. I can't believe Sutton did this either." Adam looked at me, then Yome.

"Well, that's why I'm here. I don't believe that Charlie is guilty."

"Are you kidding me?!" I jumped up from the couch. "The woman was just in my home. I saw her bruised arms and legs. I saw her beaten body. She told me it was him."

Yome stood up with me, trying to calm me down. "Laura, I know you're upset. This is why I thought it was perhaps better that you didn't attend this consultation."

Consultation? I couldn't believe where Yome was intending this meeting to go. Adam raised the question before I could.

"Frank, what consultation are we talking about?"

"Adam, please, you above all people believe in 'innocent until proven guilty'. Charlie is only accused right now. There's a lot more to this than you know."

"But Frank, this is personal. This is close."

"It is close. It's close to me, too. Charlie was my attorney before you. Before he got disbarred. You know that. You know him. You just said it yourself, that you couldn't believe he would do this."

I couldn't believe Adam was listening to Yome. He wasn't responding positively, but he had dropped back in his chair and picked up a pad and pen. He kept listening.

"There's a lot more to this, Adam. Charlie's getting set up. I want you to talk to him. He wants to see you. He needs you."

Adam's eyes shimmered with anger and dismay, shock and fear. Cords of raw, glistening energy whipped across and against his open mind. Arguments of crime and punishment strutted with theory of justice and constitutional law. Would the conviction and ultimate capital punishment of this man take away all the hurt and injury suffered by those women? And what if he's truly not guilty?

A man in a robe quickly intervened, holding a challis of wine and a scroll of mandates, ordering the release of all thoughts of defense. And Susan pushed and screamed and kicked until she tripped, knocking into the man in the robe and spilling the challis of wine. There was law. And there was a system that embodies that law. Adam saw the possibility of Charles Sutton's innocence. I knew he was going to choose to defend him.

CHAPTER 6

A transformer outside the courts building burst, leaving the entire interior of the Prosecutor's Office without electricity. There were no lights on, no computers in operation, but the minds of the office were still working. And mouths were moving. Reporters were asking questions. And they were receiving answers from Mark Weinstein.

I stood in a corner next to a couple other assistant prosecutors taking in the melee. Weinstein had met with the County Prosecutor earlier in the day, asking to be appointed special prosecutor in the Charles Sutton case. His request was granted. Currently, the reporters were discussing his return to the office and his prior successes, most notably, a string of victories in the state's highest profiled capital murder cases. Weinstein basked for a few moments in his past glory, but then turned to the matter at hand.

"Res ipsa loquitur," he told the reporters.

"Res ipsa what?" a man with a pad asked.

"It's Latin for 'the thing speaks for itself.' This entire case, its evidence, speaks for itself. The Bergen County Prosecutor's Office doesn't necessarily need me to ensure a conviction against Charles Sutton. But I'm here anyway. I'm here to see to it that this depraved piece of trash does not escape the death penalty through some legal trickery played out by his mouth piece, Adam Burr."

"You and Mr. Burr have some political, even personal, animosity, isn't that true? Is that perhaps why you came back to prosecute this case?" the same reporter questioned.

"No, it's not. I don't like Mr. Burr, it's no secret. But more important, I don't like his tactics and I don't like his lawyering. I don't want his maneuvering to cloud the issues in this case. That's why I will handle this prosecution. Not for personal reasons, but to see to it that justice is served and that Charles Sutton is punished. Severely punished."

I looked around the hallway we were standing in. It was early March, nearing five o'clock, and the area was quickly darkening. With little light, things appeared cleaner than usual. The ceilings. The walls. The doors. The floors. All cleaner. But the people were the same. Weinstein was disingenuous. This wasn't about justice and appropriately punishing Charles Sutton. It was about personally defeating Adam. And it was about politics. Shrewd politics. Mac Blaine's campaign manager prosecuting the man who raped his opponent? A reporter began a question on that topic, but abruptly stopped when he noticed Adam walking down the hall. The press raced down to see him. Weinstein followed.

Outside, a caterpillar dropped from a tree branch and fell to the ground. It sputtered around for several seconds, turning and shaking and curling up. Then it broke apart or changed or something. One color became many. And it could fly. It could fly. And it did.

Inside, Adam waved his hands as he spoke. He seemed to be pointing at the new born butterfly, showcasing its flight. But that wasn't the case. He was talking of justice and freedom and the right to be in the outside world. And he was describing wrongful punishment. I saw chains and shackles. And electricity and poisonous gas. I saw the Ghost of Christmas Past. *The death penalty?* he asked. That punishment is only reserved for murder cases. Who is doing the maneuvering here?

Back outside, a child pulled the spokes from a wheel and chitter-chattered in native dialect. The same child tossed the spokes upon the air, apparently attempting to strike the butterfly. The metamorphosised creature maneuvered with grace, dodging the spokes and spinning around the child's head. The butterfly came close to the youth's ear and whispered something of importance. The whisper was loud though, and the other children heard. They laughed raucously, pointing and jotting notes of graffiti upon the walls. The child, dismayed, ran from the butterfly and the other children and disappeared into the ever darkening night.

At this time, the lights suddenly reappeared. I looked over to Adam, and he was laughing with the reporters about something, who knows what. Weinstein was close to out of sight, waddling down the hall. Adam glanced over to him, then to me, and smiled. I smiled back. I understood his motivation for taking the case. But someone else didn't. I mouthed to him, "The Bishop."

The Bishop's meter pointed directly toward the sun. I didn't know if it was purposely placed that way or if it naturally fell to the same. The hat, reflecting the sun upon the trees, partially shaded the Bishop's face. But still, you could see the curved lines which angled at the corners of his eyes. At particular moments, the lines stood out more than others. Not because of differences in the sun or shade, but because of the Bishop's waxing emotions.

The Bishop initially greeted Adam with warmth. He hugged his nephew and made reference to his pride in him. But then he advised of his opposition to Adam's defense counsel of Charles Sutton. His face strained as he spoke of the destruction that such representation could cause to Adam's current and/or future political career. His stress seemed eased, though, when Adam responded with dialogue denoting that he too was concerned with political successes. But the problem was not resolved and the Bishop knew that. Last evening's press conference had solidified that Adam was on the case. He wanted explanations and Adam had no difficulty defending his position. The two men arose from the park bench we were sitting on and walked a few feet away to stand under a tree. There, Adam reinitiated their verbal exchange.

"Susan told me that the man who raped her, came to her from behind and pressed a chloroform soaked rag against her nose and mouth." Adam choked the tree as an example. "But the chloroform didn't work as quick as it should have because the rag wasn't flush against her nose and her mouth was closed. So she was able to see the man for a moment as she was passing out."

"And it was Sutton," the Bishop said with confidence.

Adam shook his head. "Well I'm not convinced that's who she definitely saw. I don't think she can properly identify who raped her."

"And why not? She said she saw him as she was passing out."

"Well that's not exactly how she put it to me. She said it was like a dream. That it was dark in the room. But she saw Charles Sutton's shadowy face and knew it was him from his eyes. And she said she could smell him. That's what she told me."

"You're going to use the words of a raped woman, who came to you in confidence, against her? Is that what you're about now?" The Bishop slapped the tree.

"I'm about getting to the truth, Bishop. And what Susan told me leaves a lot of doubt. It's not a positive I.D. Here, you have a woman who was passing out under the influence of knockout chemicals. A woman who was also in the dark. She sees a shadowy face of a man who had hurt her in the past? And she smelled him? What's that? You want to see a man convicted on that identification?"

The Bishop looked around for a few moments, then responded. "There's got to be more than that. Otherwise, they wouldn't have locked him up."

"Sutton's locked up because Susan told the police that he raped her. I think she really believes it was him, in her own head. But you can't prosecute a man for rape and attempted murder based on that identification. Especially when you have nothing else, in any of the cases. There's no eyewitness accounts. No physical evidence of any kind. And no confessions. Can you now tell me that there's not a ton of doubt here?"

"I'm just telling you that I don't want *you* to represent him. Find him another stalwart attorney."

"No. What if he's not guilty? What if he gets convicted and he's not guilty? Then another person's life is destroyed. I can't let life get destroyed. I couldn't as a doctor. And I won't as a lawyer."

"This is a disaster," the Bishop ignored Adam's life statement.

"Why's this a disaster?" Adam answered his own question. "It's a disaster because you want me to run in her place. That's it, isn't it? And this ruins your plans."

The Bishop put his hands on Adam's shoulders. "This is your destiny, Adam. Not just Congress. More. Much more. You're fated. Very specially fated. You know it. And you've known it for a long time now."

Adam knocked away the Bishop's hands. "I'm just a man! That's all, just a man."

"No! You're not just a man." The Bishop grabbed Adam's shoulders again. "Could just a man have done what you did in the war?"

At this last question, the conversation turned to a whisper and I could only decipher parts of what was being said. This, I do know to be true, though:

A man on a horse galloped through the countryside. A chassis of gold and silver and bronze and platinum surrounded and filled the man's torso and limbs. His armor protected not himself, but those who stood at his side. Something else, something I couldn't see, protected him. Still, even laced in these precious metals, he could not save all. There was interference of human free will. And the froth of human insanity. And the man's own need to sleep. But when these mortal properties were absent or manipulated or ortherwise removed via trickery or divine magic, the man on the horse could protect and save. And he did like no other man had before. But what of killing one man to save another or even ten others? Was that his valiant duty? Was that the work of the specially fated?

That night I laid in my bed with questions. I wanted to know more. I wanted to know exactly what happened in the war. I wanted to know exactly who Adam was. And what his plans were, or even more so, what the plans were for him. I wanted to know all these things. But more than that, I wanted to make love to him that night. So I laid in my bed. Naked. And as I wished for Adam to arrive, he came next to me. He was dressed, but only in his briefs. I ripped them down before he could lay with me, and I pulled his hands to my breasts and opened my womanhood to him. I made love to him with a passion.

CHAPTER 7

From the Bible:

I saw heaven standing open and there before me was a white horse, whose rider is called Faithful and True. With justice he judges and makes war. His eyes are like blazing fire, and on his head are many crowns. He has a name written on him that no one knows but he himself. He is dressed in a robe dipped in blood, and his name is the Word of God.

I didn't have my answers about Adam. But I did have him. I had his heart and his soul. And I had his trust. He didn't want me to be just his fiancee any longer. He was asking me to be his law partner now. To work with him and alongside him, in love and law and justice.

Pursuant to Adam's request, I resigned from my duties at the Prosecutor's Office. A resignation from a legal position is akin to a resignation from any other occupational post. Two weeks notice is customary. However, because of my superseding employment, namely a partnership with the man defending the state's most villainous individual, I was asked to exit swiftly. I had one day to transfer my cases to another assistant prosecutor and retrieve my belongings.

Leaving the Prosecutor's Office to work with Adam was an easy decision for me. At least today it was. It wasn't a new idea. It was something I thought about for over three years. Something I had pondered and considered and studied. And in the beginning, it was a notion I rejected. I wanted my independence from him. I wanted my own career. I needed time to grow as a professional and make my own passage into the barristers' world. And Adam had never asked me to work with him anyway. But now he did. And now, I had grown. I had handled over two thousand criminal matters and tried over ten cases. I had independently fostered and maintained numerous relationships with colleagues and judges. I knew the law and I knew myself. I wanted this partnership. And today, it would begin. We were meeting with Charles Sutton at the county jail.

Sutton. Sutton. Sutton, Sutton, Sutton. Something didn't sound right. It sounded wrong. Say it again. Sutton. Sutton. Sutton, Sutton, Sutton. Wrong! Wrong! Sutton. Sutton. Sutton, Sutton, Sutton! It sounded wrong. It did. There was a vowel missing or changed or something. Sutton. Sutton. Sutton, Sutton--

"Laura?" I couldn't delve into my sounds any longer. Adam was behind me, tapping my shoulder. "Laura, we've got to go. We're going to spend at minimum, an hour with Sutton."

I trembled when I heard that sound.

"What's the matter?" Adam felt me shake because his hand was still on my shoulder.

"Nothing . . .I had a chill." I didn't want to alert him of my fright of our client.

Adam began massaging the back of my neck. "I'll ease your tensions. I know this is a big step for you. Changing from one side of the law to the other. Leaving your friends at the office. Having to share a table in a jail with an accused rapist."

I turned around to stop his massaging. "I'm not tense. I'm not worried about going to the jail and sitting next to, to him."

Adam had beautiful eyes. And he spoke to me with those eyes sometimes. He just looked at me, speaking to me and massaging me with those eyes until I broke.

"Okay. I know I've supported you in taking this case. But I've thought about it and… Sutton, he's just, he's just wrong. I can feel it. Can't you?"

"It's not my job to feel whether Charles Sutton is wrong. But I do feel what I feel."

"You feel what you feel? What's that supposed to mean, Adam?"

"Let's talk about my job, our job now. As defense attorneys, our job is to win."

I interjected, "That was my job as a prosecutor too."

"No, I don't think so, Laura. A prosecutor's job is to seek

justice. Sometimes seeking justice means not winning. It means dismissing on your own motions sometimes, when you see that you don't have the requisite evidence in a case. When you feel that you can't prove your case beyond a reasonable doubt. That's what a prosecutor truly should be doing at all times. Seeking to preserve justice. And if preserving justice means winning, then with all your fervor, as a prosecutor, you should try to win. But if preserving justice means that a case should be dismissed, then you as a prosecutor, should forget about winning and dismiss that case. But we don't have that luxury of choice as defense attorneys. We can only think one way with all of our cases. And that way, is winning."

"But what about if you feel that someone is guilty?"

"Isn't that something you've thought about, Laura? Isn't this the most basic question for a defense attorney--what if you think someone is guilty?"

"But what if you think someone is guilty of the most serious, most heinous crimes? What then, Adam?"

"What then?" Adam put his hand back on my shoulder and changed from the general to the specific. "I think there's reasonable doubt in Charles Sutton's case. I think that means he should be acquitted. Because that's our criminal justice system. That's the mandate of our constitution." Adam paused and looked in the mirror opposite us. He seemed to nod to himself. "I chose to take this case. You chose to work on it with me. Now, we have to put our feelings aside. We have to look at the law. Look at the reasonable doubt. And win. That's it." Adam took his hand from my shoulder and just used his eyes again.

"Will you stop looking at me?"

The eyes.

"Stop looking at me."

The eyes.

"Come on, Adam, stop looking at me! You know you win me over with those eyes." I smiled because he wouldn't stop. "Okay, let's go to the jail." I turned away and grabbed my briefcase and pocketbook. "You're right, there is a lot of doubt in this case. Maybe it shouldn't even be prosecuted. I can't let my feelings and guesswork get in the way." I was prepared to win.

The Bergen County Jail wasn't an unfamiliar place to me. I drove by it nearly every day because it was directly behind the courthouse and Prosecutor's Office. But I had never been inside it before. I never had any reason to be. And today, even though I had a reason, I wanted the visit to be as short as possible.

The building was a rectangular institution of stone, steel and inescapable security hardware. It was set back from the street, having about two thousand feet of parking lot ahead of it. After we were buzzed into the structure by a sheriff's officer monitoring the front door, we were required to check in at a desk in the lobby. There, we provided the name of our client, as well as attorney identification. One sheriff's officer called to another, advising of our presence and then Sutton was summoned from his cell block. We were led from the lobby through a set of electronically controlled steel doors and into a hallway that housed a row of miniature attorney-client counseling rooms. Adam dropped his briefcase on the unit's lone piece of furniture, a table, which nearly collapsed when the case landed on it. He shook his head at the decrepit decor. "I'm going to another room to get us some chairs. I'll be right back." Adam kissed me and went to retrieve the chairs, allowing the room's door to close behind him.

I sat alone for a few seconds, and then the door re-opened. It wasn't Adam. It was Sutton. "The Prosecutor's Office is offering me representation now? How nice." Sutton appeared to be in fine condition in face of having spent the last few weeks in prison.

"I'm Adam's partner now," I responded. I tried to hide my nervousness by pulling my briefcase from the floor and opening it on the table.

"I figured that." Sutton looked over his shoulder, hearing the door being pushed open. Adam pulled in two chairs.

"You two sit. I'll stand," Adam told us. He pushed my briefcase to the side and lifted the top from his, removing certain items of the case's discovery. "Tell me about this." Adam dropped a packet of paperwork in front of Sutton.

The former lawyer scanned through the pages, scrutinizing selected paragraphs. He was an obviously intelligent man. But you could tell his intellect was the product of a disorder, probably a manic malfunction. "So? What the fuck's this?" Sutton handed the paperwork back to Adam.

"It's evidence Weinstein intends to use." Adam handed the packet to me.

"It's hardly relevant to this case. The probative value is certainly substantially outweighed by its prejudicial effect."

"You slept with a fifteen year old girl?" I cut in. The paperwork was the State Supreme Court's decision upholding Sutton's disbarment. The decision was held in camera, meaning that it wasn't public domain.

"Two," Sutton responded matter-of-factly.

"I thought you were disbarred for misuse of your trust account." That was the rumor.

"Nope, it was for fucking two girls. Both who consented." Sutton apparently felt consent was germane. But it wasn't. Statutory rape--an adult having sexual intercourse with a juvenile under sixteen--is a strict liability crime which ignores the issue of consent.

"Why weren't you charged criminally?" He had obviously avoided prosecution because of the lack of publicity in the matter.

"The case was initiated by both girls' parents. They had banded together and hired a private attorney who contacted me, threatening a civil lawsuit. They had no intention of having me charged criminally, because then they would lose out on their money. You know, you can't threaten criminal to get ahead in a civil case. That's extorsion." Sutton took the Supreme Court ruling from my hands.

"So what happened?" I asked.

"I paid them. I paid them a lot of money. And I thought that would be the end of it. But this prick attorney notified the bar association. He thought he was obligated to. The bastard was just trying to protect himself." Sutton folded the papers in half and continued. "So the bar investigated. And they talked of criminal charges. But the girls refused to testify and I had all kinds of language in the release where the girls denied having any sexual contact with me. But the bar didn't care. They made their own finding of fact that I was guilty of statutory rape and disbarred me. I appealed to the State Supreme Court and they agreed with the bar. Then I was prepared to appeal to the United States Supreme Court," Sutton stopped for a moment and unfolded the papers, smoothing them out with his hands. "But I didn't because I was able to strike a deal where the reason for disbarment could never be disclosed to the public. It was an unusual deal, so I took it. That's the story, Laura. And it doesn't make me a rapist, I don't give a fuck what anyone says. And it's not relevant to this case anyway."

"I'm not so sure. Rule 404(b)," Adam pulled out a green book, New Jersey's Rules of Evidence.

"I know what Rule 404(b) says. Prior bad acts are admissible in some instances. I don't think this is one of those instances." Sutton motioned for Adam to put the book away.

"Maybe it is. Maybe it isn't. But Weinstein is going to make the motion on this. He's also going to make a motion to have your blood sampled to test for HIV which I will adamantly oppose. I think that I've got a novel search and seizure constitutional argument. But I think Weinstein's got more than this, though." Adam looked directly into Sutton's eyes.

"Like what, Adam? If he's got something, he's got to turn it over to you."

"I think he's holding out. And I want to talk to you about this." Adam turned to me.

"You want to talk to me?" I knew Adam was referring to the utilization of the remainder of my day. My last day at the Prosecutor's Office. I was going to have to make a decision. A very serious decision.

There was this vision. This belief. A game was being played. But it really wasn't a game. It was real. Really like a game in its design and quality, though. Two sides, both with the intent to win. And rules. Rules that are to be adhered to by both sides. And if one side does not adhere, then it is punished. It is punished by those who oversee. But sometimes the rules can be broken, and the overseers do not see. And if they do not see, then there is no punishment and the side breaking the rules has a distinct, improper advantage. In winning. And winning, as we have discussed, is what it is all about. In a game. And in reality.

Adam knew that Weinstein was not turning over certain documentary evidence, even though the rules of discovery obligated him to provide to defense any and all evidence he had at his disposal. Adam didn't know exactly what those documents were, but he did know certain items were missing. A judge, of all people, had tipped him off. But this judge was not the same judicial officer who was presiding over Sutton's case, and he refused to involve himself any further that the information he had granted to Adam. This left us in a bind. Weinstein was breaking the rules and it surely was giving him an advantage. If we motioned the court on this missing discovery issue it would appear to be in bad faith. What evidence did we have that Weinstein was holding out? Weinstein could hold onto these documents for virtually any period of time, and then, after he had investigated their contents and drained them of all their value, turn them over to us. But, no. That wasn't going to happen. Because, here I was, rummaging through Weinstein's office.

I had gone through four milk crate size boxes marked with Sutton's name. Everything I read, we already had. Police reports. Supplemental investigative reports. Hospital records. Victim statements. Medical lab reports. Fingerprint analyses. We had all this stuff. I looked around the office for a moment, realizing it was basically empty except for these boxes.

Weinstein had no other cases, so there weren't any other files laying around. So I went to his desk. The middle drawer was locked, but it probably only held pens, pencils, paper clips and things of that sort. The two drawers on the right side, I pulled open next. They were cluttered with legal journals and different law books. But the drawer on the left side held different items. I pulled out its contents, one manila folder, and sat back in Weinstein's cheap government chair. And I drifted. . .

A talisman, a fireman, and a man of God joined hands at a picnic. They each clapped with their free hand, fingers against palm, and spoke a song in unison. The other picnickers picnicked. And they watched close, but they knew not nor did they want to know. And they didn't make a sound. Only the men in joined hands sounded. But their sound was slow, and very, very, low. Their words, to be sure, were meant to be a secret. But what's meant to be shall not always be.

The talisman ignited a flame with the man of God. It burst to the high heavens and then came back again, striking the earth and breaking its crust. The flame drilled and drilled until it reached the earth's core and then some more. At that point, a new character entered. He was dressed in red and had a tail. He spoke, but not in words, only in anger. And he pulled the flame through the core and out the earth's other end. And he attempted to take it with him. But not so. The fireman, who had appeared to be with the talisman and the man of God, broke rank, snapping his hand away and hosing a mighty water at the flame. The flame disappeared as quickly as it came. And then, the news appeared.

A middle-aged attorney with a beard had represented the Catholic Church, and his invoices were paid by a then Monsignor, John McFarlane. The attorney's representation was not limited to religious outfits, though. He also counseled a house of hell, an abortion clinic. An irony, to say the least. And low and behold, at this home of death, he met a true love--one of its clientele. An attorney and future congressional candidate,

Susan Sezman.

The Bishop had been a client of Charles Sutton. And Susan, a recipient of an abortion at a clinic that Sutton had represented. Cindy Marltana, one of the rape victims, also had aborted a child at the same location. Weinstein's notes indicated that there was more to come. . .

I dropped the manila folder and its data. Not just because of its shocking revelations, but because Weinstein's door was suddenly opening.

"Laura, what the hell are you doing?!" Weinstein flung the door open, shouting loud enough for anyone in the hallway to certainly hear him. But very few people were around. It was past six, and this was a government office.

"Nothing." I dropped the manila folder to my feet.

Weinstein ran up to me and looked at me in his chair. "Nothing? How can you be doing nothing when you are sitting at my desk? You have no business in here."

I was caught, so I determined to respond. I knew I could give a candid answer because the situation spontaneously arose and there was no way he was tape recording me. "I knew you were holding out on us, so I checked around. And guess what," I picked up the manila folder, "I found this." I placed the folder in Weinstein's hands.

"You're way out of line, Laura. You're going to lose your license for this." Weinstein's face was always a different shade. This time, pale red.

"For what?" I stood up to be eye level with his changing colors. "Prove I was in here. And if you can even do that, prove that I wasn't in your company the entire time I was in here."

"You and Adam are very dangerous people, Laura. I'm going straight to the judge with this. Straight to the judge." His face was now dark red.

I walked to the door. "When you go straight to the judge, make sure you bring that folder with you. Show him the evidence that you failed to turn over to us. I'm sure he'll understand your ignorance of the discovery rules. I'm sure he'll understand your withholding of evidence in a highly media covered criminal case. I'm sure he won't sanction you for that."

Weinstein held the folder against his chest and smirked at me. "I just got this information earlier today. It was coming to Adam tomorrow."

"Bullshit." I knew he was lying.

"Prove it, Laura. Prove it. You won't say anything about it, because you weren't snooping around in here, right? So you don't know anything about this file, right?" Weinstein dropped the file on his desk. "Adam will get this information whenever I feel like giving it to him."

"You act like you're on the right side of the law. That you're seeking justice. That you're the one that's being violated. But it's us that are being violated here. You pick and choose the rules that you want to follow. And you twist and turn the law to the way that best fits your plans. You're the bad guy here!" I grabbed the wood of Weinstein's door and whipped it against his wall.

"But to the judge, you will be the bad guy, Laura. You will be." He yelled to me as I walked away from his office.

CHAPTER 8

Short of nothing, there is something. Perhaps not much, but still something. An inkling. A morsel. A minimal amount. Nothing to be nervous about. Nothing to fret or worry over. But this wasn't a case of nothing. Not nothing at all. There was something. But just a little something, I thought. Just a little something. . . or could it be a whole lot more?!

What's the significance of Susan having an abortion? Is there relevance in the matter that the doctor who performed Susan's abortion was a client of Sutton's and that he arranged their initial meeting? Is there relevance in the fact that this same medical doctor performed an abortion for Cindy Marltana? What's more to come? Were the other rape victims also patients of his? Does this negate the randomness? It does tie Sutton in a bit closer. But only a bit. And what's the bit about the Catholic Church and the Bishop being a former client of Charles Sutton? That's not really new news. Was Weinstein preparing for a smear campaign against the Bishop? Was he now going to try to drag us all down? But don't I have something on him? His withholding of evidence. His clear violation of the rules. So is there really something in his threats to bring my little office visit before the judge? Is there something? Or is there nothing? No, this was something short of nothing. I had to get to Adam.

I pressed the clutch and downshifted so my gears would move from fifth to fourth. Then I hit the clutch again to allow a change to third gear. I cruised at thirty-five miles per hour for a minute, or maybe two, then engaged another down shift so I could safely turn into St. Anthony's parking lot. Adam had an early evening meeting with the Bishop at his private quarters. I walked into the church to get to the Bishop's residence.

Inside, there were divided walls and a centerpiece with a Godly figure. There were monuments and persons of a sort and other colorful figures. Things jumped and moved and came at

65

you. Some with a serene gesture, others with a demanding force. But there were no hellbent creatures in here. Not a demon nor a beast, nor a devil's helper. I felt that and knew it. They could come in, though. And you had to watch for that. You had to look at the divided walls.

And ask questions of the Godly figure, or at least the colorful ones. You had to decipher between trick and treat.

I wandered through the haven, but quickly. I stopped when I sensed a man. His hand was on my shoulder and his voice in my ear. I shook with the organ that was playing above.

"What's the matter, Laura?"

I turned at the Bishop. "Nothing . . .I got startled . . . I thought I would find you and Adam at your house."

"This is my house."

This is God's house. "I meant your home. Where you live."

"I know what you meant, honey. I'm playing with words." The Bishop pushed back my hair and smiled upon me. I fell upon a sudden ease.

"Adam's not here, is he?" I asked.

"No, he's not. He left almost an hour ago. He went to see Frank Yome."

"Senior or Junior?"

"Senior. Something to do with Charles Sutton's case."

I sat down in one of the pews. The seating was uncomfortable, even painful. I felt the wood vibrating and stinging against my uterus. The Bishop smiled again, trying to remedy my most recent discomfort.

"Laura, are you sure you're okay?"

"No I'm not." I stood up to speak to him.

"Well, talk to me. That's what I'm here for. To talk to you. Certainly, to all of you," the Bishop pointed around the cathedral defining his duty of service to all of his parishioners, "but even more so, to my immediate family. Every man, even a direct representative of God, has an obligation, first, to his own family. What's your worry, Laura?"

Comfort again returned. I thought it would be a treat to

divest my concerns to the Bishop. And accordingly, I began to advise of my earlier investigation and confrontation with Weinstein. "I did something today without thought. Something I thought I never would have done."

The Bishop waited for me to continue.

"I did something unethical; I guess, even illegal."

"What was it, Laura?"

"I broke into Mark Weinstein's office. Adam asked me to."

"So what you did," the Bishop turned his ring as he spoke, "something you would've never done before, was because of Adam?"

"No, yes...no...Adam's a smart man." I didn't know exactly what I meant by that.

"You're smart too, Laura."

"I don't mean it that way. I know I'm intelligent...I just mean he realizes things that I sometimes don't. And we were tricked here by Weinstein."

The Bishop continued to turn his ring. "So you weren't tricked by Adam?"

"No, why would say that? You think Adam would try to trick me?"

"No. I'm just trying to see what you think. Do you think that?"

"No, I don't--"

"Then why are you struggling?"

"I'm struggling, Bishop, because I don't know why I did this. Why I did something that could ruin my career."

The Bishop stopped turning his ring and allowed me silent introspection for several minutes. He allotted me time to gather my thoughts and realize why I actually had acted the way I did. I first had thought of Adam and the hold he had over me. But that hold wasn't powerful enough. I was a strong woman, who made my own decisions regardless of any man's will, including Adam's. The choice to invade Weinstein's office was mine. Perhaps because I wanted to win myself. Perhaps because I just wanted to impress Adam. But not because Adam made me do it.

He didn't make me leave the Prosecutor's Office and join his firm. And he didn't make me engage in unethical behavior. I made myself do it.

My thoughts turned to speech and I advised the Bishop of my conclusions. He nodded with interest, resuming with his ring turning. He permitted me ample opportunity to explain all my thoughts on this subject. When I finished, he asked me a singular question. "Who is Adam to you?"

"He's my fiance. He's the man I'm going to marry. He's the man I'm going to spend the rest of my life with."

The Bishop shook his head. "No, I mean who is he to you spiritually?"

"Spiritually?"

"Yes, spiritually."

I had always thought of Adam spiritually; even as my soul mate. But I didn't have a particular phrase or sentence to accurately define my thoughts in this manner, I guess because I was still seeking answers about him. But pinned with the Bishop's question, I had to come up with something. No, I wanted to come up with something. "Adam is the man I rise and fall with. He's the man I rise and fall with." With that, I changed topics, readdressing the issue of my trespass of Weinstein's office. And I divulged everything.

I told of the records which showed the Bishop's attorney-client relationship with Sutton. The Bishop laughed, scoffing at what he saw as a fishing expedition by an overzealous prosecutor. I then divulged the original meeting place of Sutton and Susan Sezman, and the fact that Cindy Marltana was also a patient of this same abortion clinic which Sutton had represented. The Bishop only grimaced, with no verbal response. But he did take speaking note, and actively consoled me, when I explained my fear of being sanctioned for unethical behaviors as an attorney. He promised me that he would do all he could settle to the matter in mine and Adam's favor. And then he recited a passage from the Bible to me:

I was given a reed like a measuring rod and was told, "Go

and measure the temple of God and the altar, and count the worshipers there. But exclude the outer court; do not measure it, because it has been given to the Gentiles. They will trample on the holy city for 42 months. And I will give power to my two witnesses, and they will prophesy for 1,260 days, clothed in a sackcloth." These are the two olive trees and the two lampstands that stand before the Lord of the earth. If anyone tries to harm them, fire comes from their mouths and devours their enemies. This is how anyone who wants to harm them must die.

For an hour after I left the Bishop, I drove aimlessly through North Jersey. I sped down highways and across interchanges and I rode local streets. I had no destination, no specific location to reach. I just drove to ease my mind. But finally, I found myself at The Meadowlands, the state's sports complex and entertainment center. I coasted into one of its parking lots and sat in my car, looking at the buildings.

The facility included Giants Stadium, the home ball field of both the New York Giants and the New York Jets. Why they were still called New York teams when they played in New Jersey, I don't know. But they did in fact rumble and tackle and chase the football in the Garden State. Next to Giants Stadium was an arena where the New Jersey Nets and the New Jersey Devils hosted their basketball and hockey games. Continental Arena was the name now stretched across this building, but it had previously been called Brendan Byrne Arena, after the New Jersey Governor who ordered its construction.

I found solace in looking at these two pieces of architecture. I could feel the exhilarated crowds. And I could see the athleticism and strength. Whether on ice, grass or wood court, there were always exciting battles of sportsmanship being engaged here. Triumphant and victory were sought in every matter. And to be sure, someone always won. But someone also always lost. And that bothered me. Because I was now in a battle with Mark Weinstein. And I intended not to lose.

"We're not going to lose, Laura." I jumped back, startled, although I recognized the voice.

"Adam, how did you know I was here?" *How did he know what I was thinking?*

"It's either here or the park. You always come to one or the other when you need to think." Adam was kneeling beside my car, speaking to me through my open window. I could only see his face. He looked so cute, but also concerned for me.

"You know what happened?"

Adam nodded his head yes.

"What's going to happen? Am I going to get disbarred? How'd you find out already?" I didn't know which question to ask first, so I asked them all.

Adam walked to the passenger side of my car and got in. "The Bishop called me and told me that you had talked to him. But the judge got to me first."

"And what did he say?" I was anxious.

"He said that Weinstein called him at home and accused you of breaking into his office. And he's going to hear Weinstein's accusations when he decides the other pre-trial matters in Sutton's case," Adam broke for a moment and stared at me. His manner suddenly changed. "I'm so sorry, Laura. I'm so sorry I got you involved in this. I should've just let you stay at the Prosecutor's Office."

"Adam, I'm a big girl. I make my own decisions. You didn't force me to do anything here. I just want to do damage control now...I just don't want to get disbarred."

"You're not going to get disbarred, Laura." Adam's words were soft, but confident. "Weinstein has every reason to fabricate stories against us. He's got nothing but his word, and that's nothing."

That nothing soothed me. I kissed Adam gently on the lips. "You somehow always know how to say the right things, you know that?" I kissed him again. "You know that, don't you? But you know I'm still going to worry until this is over."

"I know that." Adam motioned to the door. "Let's take a

walk over to the stadium."

"Okay." I grabbed my purse and met Adam outside the car. "Did the Bishop tell you what I found in Weinstein's office?" I took Adam's hand.

"Uh-huh."

"It's interesting material, isn't it?" I wanted his thoughts on the information.

"Uh-huh."

"Well, are you going to tell me what you think about it?"

"Uh-huh," Adam smiled just quick enough for me to not get annoyed. "I think we've got some investigating to do. Especially on this abortion clinic stuff. But our friend over here, just might have some valuable information for us right now." Adam pointed to Frank Yome who was standing next to his car. "Let's join him for some drinks."

In the back of Adam's BMW sedan was a bottle of seltzer water and a set of plastic glasses. Yome, seated by himself in the rear of the vehicle, opened the bottle with a simple twist of his wrist. In the automobile was where we were to join the organized crime head for non-alcoholic cocktails. As Adam drove well above the speed limit, Yome carefully poured three glasses of carbonated water. Adam and I held our drinks until Yome had his in hand.

"To a successful resolution of Charlie's case," Yome held up his drink. We touched glasses and then each tasted the bland bubbly.

"Is there any reason why we're drinking and driving?' I joked, but wanted to ascertain the exact purpose of this trip.

"Frank has something to show us," Adam looked quickly to Yome.

"It'll just be a few more minutes, Laura. Are you enjoying the drink? I could add cranberry juice to it, if you want."

"No thanks, it's fine, but--"

"Would you like some crackers and cheese?" Yome held up a silver plate.

"No thank you, Frank," I turned to Adam, "Not to put a

71

damper on the surprise you might have in the case, but it's been a real tough day for me."

"We're less than a mile away. Laura. I just have an address that Frank gave me. He won't tell me what this is about either."

I glanced back at Yome. This was a man who had been arrested for violating nearly every felony under statute. He couldn't understand or appreciate what I was going through. "You sure you don't want any cheese, Laura?"

I shook my head.

"Here, turn here. Turn here!" Yome pointed to a green exit sign which Adam was passing.

Adam slammed his foot on the brake pedal. The tires screeched and burned rubber against the concrete as the automobile came to an almost complete halt before the off-ramp. Then Adam slowly turned the wheel to allow us to safely exit.

"Are you sure this is necessary?" I put on my seat belt, observing the seltzer water spilled all over my blouse and skirt.

"I'm sorry, Laura. It's just over to the left." Yome pointed to a strip mall which contained several small to medium sized businesses. One of them, an abortion clinic. "Adam, park a few spots away. Not too close."

"Why?" Adam turned away from the clinic, following Yome's request before he got a response.

"Just keep away a little. No big reason."

Adam parked his car between a Chinese restaurant and a laundromat, then removed his keys from the ignition. Yome unlocked the back door and began to exit.

"Hold on, Frank. What are we doing here? This place looks closed." Adam eyed the clinic.

"No, it's not closed." Yome got out of the car.

"But what are we doing here, anyway?" I added.

"You have a right to interview any potential witnesses, don't you?" Yome smiled at Adam. "Well, I've set up a meeting for you."

Adam glared at Yome.

"Don't worry. It's a completely voluntary meeting." Yome

started toward the clinic. "Come on. Let's go."

Adam and I followed his old client into the building. Inside, we were greeted by another former client, Frank Yome, Jr., and a middle-aged woman in a white uniform.

"Hi, Dad. Adam." Frank Jr. greeted the men verbally and then extended his hand to me. "You must be Adam's fiancee."

"Yes, I've met you before." Really, I had just seen him during his trial.

"This is the nurse I told you about." Frank Jr. referred to the woman in white.

"That's correct. I'm Betty Sonderwoven. I've been a nurse at this clinic for many years. And I can tell you, that Charlie Sutton is a very, very nice man."

"Is there something else you can tell us?" Adam looked at Yome as if he were annoyed.

"Maybe," Betty answered.

"Maybe?" Yome and his son started to converge on the woman.

"Wait a minute, Frank." Adam began to laugh a little. "What do you mean, *maybe*?"

"Well, this boy here," the nurse pointed to Frank Jr., who was wearing a yellow knit sweater and eye shadow, "he's had me here for over an hour, telling me that you had something for me."

"Yeah?" Frank Sr. was agitated. I'm not sure if his displeasure was with just the nurse or his son as well.

"And he was trying to make a move on me, which I don't --"

"I don't think so," Adam cut in.

"Let's get to the point here." Frank Sr. pulled out his wallet and sifted through his large denomination bills. "This will cover it?" He handed several hundreds to Betty.

"Yeah . . .that's fine." Betty was definitely satisfied with the money count.

"Start speaking. Tell them what you told me." Frank Jr. made it a point to act hard in front of his father. Adam and I waited, interested.

"I have a few items which you might care about. One of them is that Susan Sezman was a regular here."

"What do you mean by that?" Adam asked.

"She was always here," Betty answered.

"So what. She's a pro-choice activist." Adam was prodding her.

"But she wasn't here on a mission for the cause or anything. She was just here, like with the doctor."

"The doctor's a friend of yours, isn't he?" I was checking for animosity against her boss.

"No, he's a piece of shit."

"So what are you implying? What are you trying to tell me?" Adam stood directly in front of the nurse, with his arms crossed.

"I'm just telling you she was here more than once." Betty dropped back a step. "Like when she was younger and still through older years."

"This doesn't sound like anything to me," Adam turned to Frank Sr., "Frank, ask in a gentle voice, for our money back."

"Wait, no, I have more," Betty moved closer to Adam again, touching his arm. "That Prosecutor's been here."

"Who, Mark Weinstein?" I asked.

"Yes, Weinstein, that's him."

Adam looked to Frank. "That's not any special news. Weinstein has every right to come here."

Betty touched Adam's arm again. "But does he have a right to go through our files and patient information without a subpoena? The doctor wouldn't provide anything to him."

"So how did he find out about Susan? And Cindy Marltana?"

"Well," Betty shifted her weight from leg to another, "I called him later and told him to come down."

"I thought Charles was such a nice guy?" Adam was sarcastic.

"He is. I wasn't telling anything about him. I was just giving information on that bitch. And Cindy Marltana, who the hell is

74

she to me?" Betty tried to defend herself.

"No, there's something more here. Weinstein paid you, didn't he?"

"Maybe."

The Yomes stepped closer.

"Yes, yes. He paid me." Betty put up her hands.

Adam laughed a bit again. "Well, you can have our money too."

Yome tapped Betty's shoulder, "You can have half of it." He waited until she handed a wad of hundreds back to him.

CHAPTER 9

Judge Corizan, like all others who wore the robe, was a political appointee. A former campaign contributor, who paid his dues. A party loyalist, who attended every political function and gave and gave and gave. And like most other judges, a decent attorney. Not great, but definitely above average. He had tried numerous cases early in his career, as an assistant prosecutor. Then, several more as a private practicing family law attorney. He understood the law, both criminal and civil. And he had been on the bench for over fifteen years. He was qualified to hear and decide the matter now before him and to preside over Charles Sutton's trial. Still, I didn't want this man determining my fate. I didn't think it was appropriate or fair, or just in any way, that one man alone could determine an individual's fate. But that's the way it was, at least in our system. So, here we were. In front of Judge Corizan. He had Weinstein's moving papers and was ready to hear testimony on my alleged infiltration of Weinstein's office and work product pertaining to Charles Sutton's criminal prosecution.

Adam had advised Weinstein of our little visit with Betty and that he was prepared to notify the court of his illegal gathering of evidence. Weinstein, I'm sure, had considered the gravity of the matter. Still, he hadn't yet agreed to withdraw his allegations. Adam thought, though, that Weinstein would consent to a last minute in-chambers meeting with Corizan where the matters would be washed. But there was no guarantee that would happen, so I remained concerned about the accusations against me. I clenched my fists, thinking in silence. *One person's word versus another's. One person's word versus another's. One person's word versus another's.* This was more a prayer than a thought.

I was hoping, asking, that Judge Corizan would dismiss Weinstein's charges for his lack of substantial evidence. Why should he be believed and not me? He said I was there. And I said I wasn't. *One person's word versus another's. One person's word versus another's. One person's word versus another's.*

The court room door opened and I stopped thinking. Normally, that sound wouldn't disturb my thoughts because people were always coming and going from court rooms. Lawyers. Defendants. Witnesses. Cops. Court personnel. Press. Interested bystanders. There was always an influx of people, because court proceedings were public domain. But not today. Judge Corizan had ordered a private hearing for this matter. I guess partially out of respect to Adam and me, and partially to stymie the zoo-like atmosphere which was ever growing in Sutton's case. Aside from hearing Weinstein's accusations against me this day, Corizan was rendering a decision on Adam's constitutional argument that the taking of Sutton's blood to test for HIV was an unlawful seizure, violating his Fourth Amendment rights. The press and the public were eager to hear Corizan's conclusions on that pre-trial motion. But they would have to wait. Only the lawyers involved in Sutton's case, Sutton himself, two sheriff's officers, and the judge and his staff were permitted in the court room. And that's why I stopped thinking when I heard the door open. It had to be Adam, because he was the only person who had not yet arrived.

He walked slowly from the room's entrance, almost dragging his briefcase at his side. He looked bewildered, even confused. I got up from my chair to meet him at the jury box where he had found his way to. I took his briefcase from his limp hand, and placed it at his side.

"What's wrong, Adam? What's wrong?" I didn't know what to expect.

"Mr. Burr? Is something the matter?" Corizan spoke from the bench.

Adam picked up his briefcase and walked to counsel table. He dropped the case upon the wood surface and opened it. The top part of the leather carrying case held in a perpendicular position to its body, standing straight up. It shielded Adam from the judge who was growing impatient due to Adam's lack of response.

"Mr. Burr? Whenever you are ready."

I pulled my chair closer to Adam and grabbed his hand which had now grown firmer. "Adam, what's the matter?" I whispered.

"Mr. Burr?" Corizan was now standing. "Is there something wrong?"

Adam shut the top of his briefcase and stood to face the judge. "Yes, Your Honor, there is something wrong. Something terribly wrong." Adam looked in the direction of the holding cell which was connected to the courtroom. And then at Weinstein, who was snickering in his chair.

"Well, please advise us." Corizan motioned with his gavel.

"Frank Yome and his son were murdered this morning. Their bodies were just found in the basement of Frank Sr's office. The father was decapitated. His head was sitting in a plastic basket next to his dead body. Blood was everywhere. And Frank Jr," Adam looked to me as if he didn't want to speak in my presence any longer, "Frank Jr had his genitals removed. They were stuffed in his mouth. 'Homosexual' was painted in blood on the basement wall." Adam looked down to the floor.

Weinstein, who had been sitting quietly, now stood to speak. "Well that's a very sad story. Two pillars of the community killed in, I guess, cold blood."

"Mr. Weinstein," Corizan rapped his gavel against his desk. "There is no need for your sarcastic remarks. Those were two clients of Mr. Burr's. And that kind of killing, no matter who it is--"

Corizan suddenly stopped mid-sentence and turned, as we all did, toward the holding cell. A tremendous clanging of metal sounded from the petite jail. And then we heard a blasting of gunfire. Corizan, his law clerk and the stenographer ran from the judge's bench to his chambers. Weinstein jumped from counsel table and headed for the door, but was cut down by a spray of bullets. At least four shots hit him in the upper back and neck.

Sutton ran to the door and locked it. He screamed to all who may be outside it. "Anybody who tries to come into this court room will immediately be killed. The two living people in here will be killed as well." Sutton then walked over to Adam and me. "Laura, go to that door and say a few more words for me." He was unusually calm for having just killed three people. Two sheriff's officers lay dead next to the holding cell. Weinstein's corpse, straddled over a court room bench.

"Charles, what the hell are you doing?!" Adam looked at the dead bodies, noticing a gun missing from one officer's holster.

Sutton twirled the handcuffs dangling from his one free hand and pointed the weapon at me with his other. "Laura, kindly walk over to that door and speak as I told you." He was still calm.

I looked at Adam, who no longer appeared bewildered, but now angry. "Laura, don't do anything, except walk to that door, unlock it, and leave."

Sutton wielded the gun, pointing it first at me, then at Adam, then back at me again. "Laura, go to the door now and do as I say, or I will fucken blow holes through your body."

I quickly jogged from where we were standing to the door. Sutton kept the gun on me. "Now scream as loud as you can, that you and Adam are alive and that I will be in touch via phone soon."

I hit the door with my fist and then yelled, "I am alive in here. So is Adam Burr. We haven't been shot. Charles Sutton is holding us at gun point. He will accept a call soon."

Sutton waved me back with the pistol. When I reached him, he pointed to the chairs at counsel table. "Sit, the both of you. Let's talk. Let's talk about Frank Yome, one of my closest friends. And let's talk about your uncle, Bishop John McFarlane," Sutton lit a cigarette, "But first let me tell you a little story. Something that makes me feel nice." Sutton's eyes blackened. And his hair shimmered white. I thought his heart had stopped, but that couldn't have been the case because he was still breathing. The phone began ringing, but he ignored it.

Instead of answering it, Sutton sat back, relaxed, in a chair at counsel table. He propped his feet up, continuing to point the pistol at us and told an insane criminal's story. I remember it, uninterrupted.

The dislike I had for Chad was not grounded in racism or ethnic separatism. Nor was it the product of any religious dispute. I just didn't like the man. I didn't like the way he talked, the way he moved or the way he looked. And his teeth, they were corroded. They weren't white or even off-white. They were yellow and blacked out in the gums. Maltreated, unclean teeth, the benchmark of white trash. I knew right from the beginning-- Chad had to go.

The elimination of Chad, though, was not a decision I could make on my own. I had to consult my partner. You see, I'm a business owner. The proprietor of a rather prestigious manufacturing outfit. On the surface, it appears that I am solo in my ownership. However, this is due to fact that I am the managing partner in this business. I handle the day-to-day operations. I oversee the billing, the collecting, the sales, the purchasing, the productivity. I do the banking. The payroll. The marketing. I do the hiring. I do it all alone. But never the firing. That's a decision for the both of us. Igor would never let me handle that task alone. And why should he? He's the man behind it all. He's the man with the money. Why should he be left out of the firing?

So I consulted with Igor. I began with the teeth. He agreed right away--Chad didn't sound good. But he wanted to know more. He wanted other specifics. Other qualitative malfunctions. The list was lengthy, but on cue, I initiated my enumeration:

Greasy hair;
Dirt in his fingernails;
Unshaven face;
Noticeable scar tissue;
Hair in his ears;
Bowlegged;

Long toe nails;
Uncircumcised.

It was at my last enunciation that Igor stopped me. He stopped me because he knew. He knew I had erred. I didn't exactly wait to consult Igor. I mean, I did consult him, because there I was, speaking to him about how to handle Chad's termination. I just had begun the process a little bit before my discussion with him. This, he didn't fancy.

I shriveled in fear for a moment, watching Igor's brow crinkle and his hand raise. The blow to my head was powerful, but disarming. The fact that he had failed to procure a weapon for his unleashing of punishment meant that my error of judgment was not grave in his calculation. Accordingly, he handled me with judicious discretion, only physically pummeling me to the dirt and fornicating in a manner about me, which to all who did not understand, was atrocious. But I understood, and I accepted the assault with brave obedience.

Igor laid me to rest with one final blow and then dug into his coat breast pocket. He removed a dark plastic bag which held inside it, an even darker looking vegetation. I watched from the floor as he stuffed his smoking pipe with apple tobacco, put fire to the same and then joyfully inhaled. It was at this time that he allowed me to stand and clean up. My infraction had been treated, so we could move on. I showered quickly and freshened with Igor's special powders and oils. I parted my hair, to the side, and then presented myself back to my partner to finish the decision-making process that we had begun merely an hour earlier.

I explained to Igor where Chad was currently located. That he was at our old warehouse, the one off the highway, far off the highway. The one that has many playful toys. Toys which we had collected over time which had come from far off times. You see, Igor and I are Renaissance Men of sorts. Medieval in nature, but I truly think not evil at all. I mean, what kind of name is Chad anyway? Shouldn't he be where I had him? Locked in a vise, halfway through a surgical procedure.

Once Igor and I had come to an agreement regarding Chad's fate, we departed for Blauchouse, the warehouse aforementioned. Blauchouse generated fond and wonderful memories within me. It was a structure of character, not necessarily in building design, but in moral value building. It was a place of human charity. A place of giving...and of receiving. I, myself, had learned the milk of human kindness there.

Igor embraced me before our entrance into Blauchouse. He quietly reminded me of the rules and kissed my forehead and cheek. The doors were always open, we never shunned visitors. So a simple push of the knobless wooden barricade was all Igor needed to do to allow us to arrive inside our palace of Blauchouse.

Chad's unwillingness to provide a friendly welcome immediately reminded me of his teeth. To remedy my discomfort and Igor's growing anger, I went to the treasure chests which sat directly to the right of Chad's incarceration. I trolleyed past the first of these rectangular units and went to the second. Upon opening the same, I procured the one item that lay within it. A handcrafted, buffed and polished solid black sporting instrument. A baseball bat. With reserve, I grasped the swinging stick and careened it off Chad's skull. Specifically, I cracked the bat across his face, knocking out at least four of those grotesque bony orbitals from his mouth.

Like the lack-of-man he was, Chad cried out and whimpered. His contorted, vised body and half-dangling scrotum only accentuated his womanhood to me. I could tell Igor was equally discouraged with Chad's inability to learn and suffer as a prideful man. My thoughts were confirmed as I watched him proceed to the third chest.

Outside, the smell of wild sunflower and dampened fallen multi-colored leaves irritated my nostrils, sending me into a panic of distress and despair. I wouldn't let it show, though. I knew I could cleverly disguise it so Igor wouldn't be apprised.

I kept one eye on him, closely monitoring as he chiseled away at Chad's limbs. With my other eye, I looked into the heavens, spotting the angels and the other characters floating effortlessly in the winds. But my eyes weren't enough. They never were. So I sought the aid of the canals in my head that allowed me to hear the whispers down below. Through them, I derived peace and comfort and was provided with directives.

Igor, at this point, had managed to saw away several of Chad's toes and currently was relieving him of his tongue. Our employee, which he still was, because technically we hadn't fired him yet, was nearly unconscious. And that wasn't right. The whispers had just told me that. And I told Igor that. And Igor laughed at me, ignoring the whispers' words. And he continued with the terror. And Chad was convulsing and slobbering at the mouth and screaming and crying. And I couldn't ignore the whispers. I grabbed Igor by the roof of his mouth and slammed him to the ground. With a heavy wooden mallet, I smashed open his head and crushed his brains with my bare feet. He died easily and that made me feel good.

Chad was then told he could go. He decided to stay, though, I guess because he couldn't move. So I made a call for help for him. And then I sat back, with Igor's pipe in hand, and thought about what I had just done. It was simple and clear. It wasn't that I didn't respect Igor's decision. And it wasn't that I disliked Igor. The truth is, I loved him. And I really did dislike Chad. But the whispers had intervened and laid out destiny. Chad had learned. The teeth, the toes, the head, the manlihood, had all been touched, treated and cleansed. He was a revitalized man. So why then should he be exterminated? Firing is one thing, but extermination is a whole other, isn't it? Well, at least that's the question the whispers raised. Igor didn't adhere. I did hear. And when there's a conflict between here and there, there rules.

You see, my decisions are not based in any prejudices or hatred. On the one end, they're just the result of likes and dislikes, preferences if you will, which I have learned from my teachers--see the case of Chad. But on the other end, they're the following of direct commands, commands that no man can ignore. That's why my most endeared teacher, Igor, had to go and Chad had to be let go. Now that's understandable, isn't it?

Sutton laughed raucously, knowing that he had told us the total story of the selected passages left with the rape victims. "Igor and Chad aren't real, in case you're wondering. But what is real, and what should be real important to you, is that today this is my Blauchouse."

Adam jumped from his seat almost simultaneously with the completion of Sutton's last sentence. "Let my fiancee out of this hell!" Adam looked around at the dead bodies. Sutton met Adam, not with a verbal response, but with his weapon. He pressed the barrel of his gun underneath Adam's chin and eased him back into his chair. Sutton's eyes continued in their blackness and his heart--his heart could not have been beating. But he smiled, so it was. And he started to speak again, discarding his story for what apparently was present business.

"So he got rid of Yome, our long time friend, huh?'

"Who's *he*?" Adam questioned.

"Who's he? You think I'm stupid?" Sutton looked from Adam to me. "You think I'm crazy, don't you? Insane? A bit bothered at least?"

We didn't answer.

"I am!" Sutton shot up. "But I'm not stupid." He walked from the center of the table to its most westerly end, and then placed his palms down, but kept his middle finger pinned against the trigger. "Your man works methodically, with the least risk. He thinks first, to just let the criminal justice system handle everything. That I'll probably be acquitted, right?"

Sutton looked directly to Adam. "There's no evidence against me, right? You, the best defense attorney around, are defending me, right? No one will talk. Not me, not Yome, so everything's alright then, right?--Well, I guess not, because now Yome's dead and his son's balls are stuffed in his mouth."

Sutton grabbed one of Weinstein's yellow legal pads and whipped it at Adam. "Your man's the one who's been in control of all this. He must have thought Frank was going to break about bringing me the money. He'll come for me now, you know that. I know you know that. That's why I'm not sitting in that jail cell waiting to be acquitted. Because he'll find a way to get to me next."

"Let Laura go, Charles." Adam refused to respond to Sutton's absurd accusations.

Sutton came forward to Adam and pressed the barrel of the gun against his face again.

"Yeah, Adam. I'll let her out. I have no need for women any longer. This will be between you and me." Sutton unbuckled his pants and let them fall below his knees. Then he pulled the 9mm from Adam and turned to me. "Go, Laura, go."

I grabbed Adam's arm and looked to him for guidance. "Get out of here Laura. I'll be okay."

Tears of fear and confusion trickled down my cheeks. I didn't want to leave Adam alone with that maniac. Perhaps the two of us would have a better chance of overtaking him. Perhaps I should stay. Adam wouldn't allow me the opportunity, though. He ripped my hand away from his arm and in almost the same motion uplifted me from the chair by my chest. "Get out of here!" With that, I darted to the door, unlocked it and retreated to safety.

Outside the court room, there was an enormous congestion of law enforcement personnel. Sheriff's officers. Local police. Prosecutors and investigators. State police. FBI. They all had the same questions. Who was still alive? What kind of weaponry did Sutton possess? Approximately how many rounds of bullets had he expelled? What was Sutton's demeanor? What did he want? Where he was standing or sitting?

Sniper units had been deployed to nearby buildings, hoping for a clear shot. But thus far, Sutton had avoided their scopes. Other police were planning a forced entry, with tear gas and fire power. And still others were hoping to negotiate a peaceful end to the murdering siege as it was now just a hostage situation. Adam's screams from inside negated, at least for the moment, one of the plans. "Don't come in! Don't come in! Don't come in!"

I burst out into tears when I heard his pleas. Friends of mine from the Prosecutor's Office attempted to console me by moving me away from the scene, but I refused their efforts. I demanded to stay close by. Adam was my fiance and I was a part of this terror. I wasn't leaving until it was over, no matter what the outcome.

An FBI agent holding a portable phone summoned me. He began asking the same questions I had already answered. I didn't care about the repetition, though. I just wanted Adam free and alive. This agent was most concerned with what Sutton may want in order to release Adam. But his questions were for naught.

A lone shot rang from the courtroom. With it, a parade of police officers crashed through the room's entrance to find Charles Sutton dead. A single bullet hole in his forehead marked his just demise.

Adam walked from Sutton's Blauchouse without assistance. He bypassed the FBI agents, sheriff's officers and other police, and fell into my arms. He whispered to me that no one was to know what happened in there. And then, in a corner of the courthouse, he told me.

Two men, and two men alone, came together. By the choice and force of one, and not the other, a matter of indignity was embraced. A serpent, disguised as one of the men, extended its arrow and pierced an untouched ground. The other man, who also was not just a man, could not fight the arrow as death as a human was the only other choice.

Sutton fornicated in a manner about Adam, which to all who did not understand, was atrocious. But I understood. Adam accepted the assault with brave obedience. He allowed it to happen, to allow me to live, and to allow that his ultimate destiny be reached.

CHAPTER 10

From the Bible:

Then I saw a new heaven and a new earth, for the first heaven and the first earth had passed away, and there no longer was any sea. I saw the Holy City, the new Jerusalem, coming down out of the heaven from God, prepared as a bride beautifully dressed for her husband. And I heard a loud voice from the throne saying, "Now the dwelling of God is with men, and he will live with them. They will be his people, and God himself will be with them and be their God. He will wipe every tear from their eyes. There will be no more death or mourning or crying or pain, for the older order of things has passed away."

The media's initial reaction to the court room tragedy was mixed. In one light, Adam was again a hero. He risked his life to save mine. And he brought to justice the murderer, Sutton. He killed a man whom he was trying to save from the death penalty. It was ironic, to say the least. And the irony is what the press blasted Adam for. Here was Adam Burr, a war hero, a medical doctor who had saved so many young lives. And now all his critics were right, especially Weinstein who was now dead-- Adam Burr was in fact defending a guilty man. He was defending a man guilty of rape, a man guilty of infecting innocent women with the HIV virus! A man guilty of senseless, inexcusable murders. But this was the media's *initial* reaction. It all changed with the autopsy results.

Charles Sutton was not HIV positive. He did not have the virus. And if he did not have the virus, he could not have infected the women. And if he did not infect the women, he was not the rapist. And if Sutton was not the rapist, then Adam Burr was indeed defending an innocent man! An innocent man, who, under all the pressures of false accusations and wrongful imprisonment, went insane. And Adam, put in yet another position of war, a position without choice, had to lay the man to rest. There was no question now, by anyone, that Adam Burr was again a hero.

Things were funny, though. Adam didn't agree with the newspaper and television correspondents. He didn't see himself as a hero. Yes, he had saved my life. And yes, Sutton's blood came up negative for HIV. But he knew Sutton was a rapist. And he knew Weinstein's notes were right--there was more to come. Much more.

Adam rolled from one end of the bed to the other. He hadn't slept for more than a couple hours every night for the past week. He was tired, but restless. He had to act.

"Laura, I'm going to see the Bishop." Adam hadn't talked to the Bishop, or anyone for that matter, since Sutton's attack.

"When?" I asked with concern.

"Tonight, after evening mass." It was Saturday and the Bishop always held five o'clock mass at St. Anthony's.

"What are you going to talk about?"

Adam moved to the edge of the bed, where he sat up and spoke from.

"There's insanity here, Laura. There's murdering, killing, raping. One man against another. There's insanity and killing everywhere. There always has been and there always will be."

The battle wounds were open and the fires were burning. Adam's eyes were burning blue with them. His dark skin radiated when he spoke. "Years ago, in the wilderness, I saw it all. Killings of all kinds. Men would butcher each other with bullets and bombs and knives and even chemicals. Some men would even butcher themselves...I watched as the cream of insanity dribbled from a man's lips, and across his cheek, and then down his chin. The insanity came from his own mind. And it went into his own hand. I watched this man thrust a knife into his neck. His blood spilled upon all of us...His sins too," Adam paused to run his hands through his hair, "I saw true, raw insanity there. And I told myself, it was just there. I told myself it was just there, Laura. But I was wrong. There's true insanity,

90

true evil, everywhere. Sinning is in all of us."

Adam got up from the bed and walked to the bathroom. "I'll be at St. Anthony's after five."

From morning until afternoon, I paced through our home, attempting at points to carry out little chores. But I was distraught with images of the dead sheriff's officers and Weinstein. Their bullet torn clothing. Their lifeless bodies. Their *blood*. Blood had spattered to my lips from Weinstein's pierced neck. I had blocked out my impulsive reaction of touching my tongue to my lips, tasting human blood. I gagged, remembering the unsavory taste.

I blocked out the images again and thought about Adam and his upcoming visit with the Bishop. I wondered what would happen, what he would learn and whether I should go. He implied that I should attend. But that meeting wasn't until after five, so I decided to take a ride.

I drove only through one county, but over three different highways. From Route 3, I exited onto Route 17 and then onto the Garden State Parkway. I traveled north on that road until I reached Exit 168, where I made my way into an affluent town which bordered New York State. After passing several quaint shops and a few ethnic restaurants, I found myself in a wholly residential zone. Large beautiful houses separated by enormous well trimmed green lawns seemed to exist only for sightseers and dreamers of wealth. But they were owned and occupied indeed. One of them by Susan Sezman.

At 104 Old Chimney Lane, I came to a stop, recognizing Susan's house from my past visits. I remained in my car for a few minutes, getting my thoughts together and preparing my questions. Inside that house, I was determined to have a trial. There would be no motions or opening statements, however. Nor the benefit of a judge and jury. Just me and my witness, who I would be carefully cross examining.

I knew Susan was upset and demoralized by recent assertions that she had concocted the entire rape story to explain

91

how she was HIV positive. There were all kinds of rumors in the tabloids ranging from labeling Susan a heroin addict to a participant in wild orgies. Her torrid love affair with Sutton was referenced more often as well as her supposed motive to name him as the rapist. Foes pointed to her well known animosity toward Sutton for his infidelity and ultimate termination of their relationship. I didn't believe in any of that, though. But I did think there was more to the story which Susan hadn't yet shared. So I resolved to ask the right questions. Susan knocked on my window, however, preventing any further trial preparation. Susan had apparently been watching me from her yard.

"Laura, do you want to come in?" Susan actually was smiling. I guess there was comfort in the company of misery.

Looking at the house and the terrors I knew Sutton had brought there, I changed my mind. "No. No thank you. Can we stay outside? It's a beautiful day."

"Yeah, of course." Susan stepped away from the window to allow me to get out of my car. I exited without moving the keys from the ignition and stepped to the curb to start my questioning. Susan spoke first, though.

"Charles may not have been HIV positive, but he did rape me. He did, I'm telling you that."

"I know he did."

"You do?" Susan was surprised.

"Yes, I do. I don't have all the answers of what happened with you and the other women. But I do have some questions that will help me get there." I was nervous to begin.

"Well ask, Laura. Ask."

I asked. And I learned. I learned more than I wanted.

At six o'clock on this Saturday, St. Anthony's looked the same as it did every sixth day of the week at this time. A powerful structure in the shadows of dusk with colorful windows and crosses and figures beaming out at the thinking people leaving an inspirational mass told by Bishop John McFarlane. One man was walking in as the others walked out.

I ran up to him, clutching his arm before he could enter.

"Susan had two abortions."

Adam looked at me, but said nothing.

"Her first abortion was at nineteen. The father of the child--"

Thunder broke out with lightening and a sudden splash of rain. Adam turned the arm grasp to his favor and pulled me into the dry church. We contacted physically with a man who was standing alone beyond the doorway.

"The father of that murdered child was me." The Bishop removed his meter, placing it atop the Holy Water.

Adam still said nothing. I wanted to leave. I wanted to stay. I stayed.

"Susan is a murderer. Charles Sutton is a murderer. Frank Yome is a murderer. You, my son, are a murderer." The Bishop touched Adam's face. "We're all murderers. Just some of us are murderers for the Word of God. Isn't that right, Adam? Tell your fiancee that it's right."

Adam looked upon me. There was no emotion in his face. Not anger. Not sadness. Not fear. "There is no murdering that is right, Laura."

"Yes there is, Adam. Killing in self defense. Killing to save others! That is right!" The Bishop pulled Adam from his look upon me.

"Killing, yes Bishop. Killing, at times may be right as it may be a necessity. But not murder. Never murder."

"Are you calling me a murderer, Adam?"

Adam didn't respond as he knew the Bishop was going to talk.

"Do you want me to confess my sins to you? It's right for me to confess my sins to you, isn't it?"

Adam stared away, toward a statute of the Mother of God.

"Well let me tell you what I did." The Bishop stepped in front of Adam's gaze. "I did what Our Father wanted. I used evil to punish evil. I played the devil and beat him."

"What did you do, Bishop?" I had the nerve to talk because Adam wasn't.

"What exactly did I do, Laura? I'll tell you exactly what I did. I went to Charles and I told him of my needs. And he told me of his needs. And we formed a plan. We spoke of the matters only once and then the work began. I had that monster paid a lot of money to punish those women who murdered children." The Bishop took hold of my hand and I couldn't pull it away. "You understand, they're murderers of children who never had a chance to live God's gift. These women needed to be punished by me because our criminal justice system won't do it."

Adam broke the Bishop's grasp of my hand. "Isn't that punishment then left for God?"

"Yes, upon their deaths. But first, they must be punished here on earth just like any other criminal. Just like any other murderer and sinner against God. I carried out God's work here. And I carried it out very cleverly, with great precaution. And with the ultimate result benefitting you and your destiny."

"My destiny? Are you sure you really want to know my destiny, Bishop? And yours as well?" Adam warned his uncle.

"Yes. Together we will prosper to the highest of posts. God's orders will see to it that I am his greatest voice on this earth. From Bishop to Cardinal to Pope. And that you become the President of this great nation, leading the misguided, confused peoples with all your divine gifts."

"So that's why Susan had to be out of the way. To get me started, right?"

"Exactly. My plan was so perfect in its twofold design. Susan, that whore, needed to be punished for aborting those children. One of them, my child...And she needed to be out of the way so you could rightfully win that congressional seat." The Bishop picked his meter off the Holy Water and held it in his hands. "This hat will be replaced by another. Your prospering will help my prospering. And in return, my prospering will help yours. You need to win that seat. And after all that has happaned, you being a hero again, you will surely be victorious."

Adam shook his head at the Bishop. "No."

"There is no 'no', Adam. This was all planned so perfectly. Charles broke into a medical lab at Princeton and heisted several test tubes of HIV infected blood. Then he took lists of women from that abortion clinic he had represented." The Bishop rubbed his hands together and nodded his head. "So we knew we would only be punishing guilty women...And Charles raped them and then injected the contaminated blood into their vaginas." The Bishop nodded his head again. "You see, he appeared to be a serial rapist, only raping women with blond hair and at seven year intervals. And it ended just right, with our target, Susan Sezman, being the last victim. It was the perfect way to get her out of the race and to pay her back for aborting my child. To punish her for her sins," the Bishop paused, reflecting for a moment, and then continued, "And Charles, he had his own reasons to punish her. None of which I cared about. But he, as you can see, was the best man for job. Remember, evil punishing evil. Perfect."

"But things really didn't go perfect, did they Bishop? Sutton got caught and then I represented him."

"Are you kidding me, Adam? Through you, I could monitor the case and stay close to things. I wanted you to represent him. I wanted you to turn your back on Susan. I wanted you to win this case for me. And for you. And I knew you would win. There was no evidence against Charles. Eventually Charles' blood would've been tested, and it would come out that he was not HIV positive." The Bishop smiled a proud fatherly smile. "Charles was going to be acquitted and you were going to come out a shining star for once again representing an innocent man." The Bishop threw up his hands and his smile turned to a mild laugh, "But things, because God was watching over ever so closely, came out even more perfect than that. Charles murdered that pain in the ass Weinstein. And then God put you in a position to act on your heroic gifts and kill Charles." The laugh stopped and the Bishop nodded with a momentous manner. "Now we have, in the end, good punishing evil on earth."

"What about Yome, Crazy John?"

The Bishop cracked a smile again. I'm not sure if it was in response to the mention of Yome or Crazy John. "Yome, well he had a part in this. But not a big part. He was just a bag man. He brought cash to Charles on my behalf, thinking I was using Charles in a stock fraud scheme. Something I had done in the past to raise money to assist in my Church promotions," the Bishop raised his hands toward the cathedral ceiling. "But that dummy didn't know what was really going on. He never tied it all together. When Charles got arrested, Yome genuinely thought he was innocent. He thought Charles was the perfect frame candidate for the rapes. He had the past trouble and he had the history with Susan...But Frank, he started doing too much personal investigation. He was getting too involved and Weinstein was closing in," he shrugged his shoulders, "I don't know what could have happened. Who knows, even a guy like Frank Yome could've broke. So he had to go. He had to be executed to preserve God's plans. Frank was a bad man, anyway."

"And what about his son?" Adam still displayed no emotion.

"Well, he was a homosexual. Clearly, it was in the interests of God to kill him."

"Well let me explain something to you," Adam pointed at his uncle, "I had anal intercourse with Charles Sutton."

"What?!" The Bishop knocked his hat from the Holy Water, causing water to splash outward and land on his feet. It burned the hollow man who no longer had the ability to speak or move.

Adam bent down to the floor and wiped the Holy Water from the Bishop's shoes. He licked the liquid from his fingers and then went to the challis holding the remainder of the water. He picked up the pot and drank its contents. Then he reached into his coat and pulled a pistol from his waist. He pointed the weapon at the Bishop and spoke in the most serene manner I had ever heard him. "I'm not just a man, you were right. I was the very first man. And I will be the very last. I'm a man who's good and who's evil. A man who's strong. And weak. As a man, I have sinned like all others."

I thought for the few moments I had left with Adam about his sins and learnings as a man.

For years, he had traveled. Sometimes alone, but more often in groups. He had tasted the flavors of life, embracing its duality of hollow body and body of soul. He had intertwined intimacy in both positive with negative and positive with positive. He had shared in laughter and in love and struck out in sorrow and in anger. His passions for the tastes of wine and the miracles of water had fruited for him a cascade of knowledge and scholarly successes. He never knew what it was all about, though. His journeys. His experiences. His learnings. Nothing had showed him. His tenure in the militia, however, brought about his realization. It was there, were he learned of killing.

Adam looked to me one final time and then to the Bishop. He kept his gun raised and spoke. "I am in the wilderness again. At war, as I have always been. While I once thought that I could save, I realize now that I cannot...I see through you, and I see through myself, that man will never stop sinning. I have killed in the past, Bishop. And now it's my time to reach my real destiny and kill again."

Adam fired the gun at the Bishop. Bullets sprayed in every direction known to man. High and low. North, south, east and west. To all corners and areas of the earth. As the fire blasted across the world, Adam cried out, alone as he was. "It couldn't work! It can't work! From day one to day last, I couldn't work it out. Nor could she. Nor could they. None of us can ever be what we are suppose to be. Never."

So by his choice, by his singular determination, they all died. The evil. The good. The weak and the strong. The men, the women and the children. All of them. In one blast of immortal order and seizure, the entire lot of human invention was annihilated.

Today, in the wasteland, it is over. For the third and final time, he leaves for home. He leaves as man. And returns home as man's maker.

ABOUT THE AUTHOR

Newspaper and television media have called Kenneth Del Vecchio *The Next John Grisham, Renaissance Man - A Profile of Success* and *Jack of All Trades, Master of All.* At only 31 years old, Kenneth Del Vecchio has already reached several amazing accomplishments:

1. **Film Producer/ Actor** - wrote, produced and played one of the lead roles in *Rules (for men)*, a full-length feature film which won *Best Comedy* at the *Atlantic City Film Festival.* The film's stars include Jackie "The Joke Man" Martling (*The Howard Stern Show)*, Vincent Pastore (*The Sopranos)*, Frank Gorshin (*Batman's Riddler)*, Jerky Boy Kamal and NYC Z-100's Christine Nagy. The film will be released nationwide in February 2001:

2. **Published Novelist** - author of criminal suspense novel, *Pride & Loyalty*, which has sold thousands of copies nationwide via Barnes & Noble and other chains;

3. **Attorney** - in 1995, became one of the youngest lawyers in New Jersey state history to win a criminal jury trial; currently serves in dual roles of criminal defense attorney and municipal prosecutor and has tried over 150 cases to date;

4. **Newspaper Editor** - served as political editor for *The Italian Tribune News,* the nation's largest Italian-American newspaper;

5. **College Teacher** - taught college classes in criminal justice and is certified to teach secondary education in New Jersey;

6. **Competitive Weight Lifter** - bench presses over 400 pounds while weighing under 165 pounds and has won numerous competitions.

Currently, Kenneth Del Vecchio is in pre-production for the film version of his novel *Pride & Loyalty.* He will serve as the film's producer and it will feature several Hollywood stars.